A Layman's view

MW01193259

WHAT EVERYONE SHOULD KNOW

ABOUT

THE HOLY BIBLE

LEN GONGOLA

SON BEAM PRISON MINISTRIES, INC.
P.O. BOX 372832
SATELLITE BEACH, FLORIDA 32937

Published by Son Beam Prison Ministries, Inc.
Satellite Beach, Florida 32937

Trademark —"Ambassadors for Christ in prisons"

Copyright ©   1993 by, Leonard (Len) V. Gongola

First printing   1993

Seventh printing 2003

ISBN 0-9671919-0-4

TABLE OF CONTENTS

ABOUT THE AUTHOR

Len Gongola began his study of the Holy Scriptures in 1975. Recognizing his illiterate condition as it applied to the Holy Bible, he made and kept a five-year commitment of special studies to become a lay minister. Having served in both teaching and preaching, when called upon, he found great joy in helping others and desired to share those things that he had learned. As with many servants of the Gospel of Jesus Christ, he believes God has already supplied the words of truth. Servants merely give testimony through their own words to the authenticity and power of God's written Word. He believes exactly what the Bible declares—the Holy Spirit of God is the only revealer of truth from the written Word. Len was ordained in October 1998.

After several years of visiting the incarcerated, the author decided to write and present a clear, concise, and straightforward book, which would tell about the love and mercy of our great and mighty God. This book would not only be a testimony of what he had learned, but would provide a sensible and balanced view of the Holy Scriptures—to help others to come to know what God has promised them too.

Retired from an industry which supplies finished and unfinished materials to various building trades, he now committed himself to supply something much greater and more important to life—truth from God's Word. He believes that anyone who will give a little of their time to read this book, will come away with a greater appreciation and knowledge of God's grace and mercy.

He believes in the exactness of what Paul told the Galatians (2:20) that his sins were also crucified at the cross of Christ and God remembers them no more. And, that his life is centered through faith in the person of Jesus Christ who died for him because of his love for all who will believe.

He believes in the exactness of what is written in the book of Hebrews (10:19-25). Those who believe in Christ's resurrection and obey him—have direct access to God. He believes even as it is written,

iv

that Christ Jesus is the great high priest who is over the House of God. And, that it is with a sincere heart in full assurance of faith that all true Christians have been cleansed from a guilty conscience.

ACKNOWLEDGMENTS

Recognizing the following friends is a pleasure. You probably do not know them, but their respected opinions, encouragement, and statements have had an impact upon this book. The author expresses his sincere thanks to:

Pauline Gongola, my wife, great supporter and friend, who said, "Many will come to know Christ as Savior."

Lawrence Gilmore, Church Elder, an encourager who never quit.

Timothy Baird, gave me my first passage of Scripture, John 3:16.

Charles George, home with the Lord, and no doubt was God chosen to encourage me to teach the Bible in the early seventies.

A heartfelt thanks to Nancy Green, Belva Fox, Madonna Howard, and Ed Lacy, for their part in making this book possible.

Every reader will appreciate the talents of A.J. (Tony) Rossi. His electronic publication technique has made this book easy to follow and help sustain continuity in reading.

To Reverend Gary Sims, Director of Prison Fellowship of Ohio, I extend my special thanks not only for his dedication and commitment in his life's work to the incarcerated and their families, but also to his never ending support in presenting this book. It is good to be associated with such a committed servant of Jesus Christ.

The author also wishes to give thanks to and acknowledge those who have read the pre-published copy of this book. Their suggestions had a definite impact on the finished work of this book.

They are: Ann Crane, Rick and Diane Raggsdale, Richard Stafford,

John Kelley, Robert and Doris Shaw, Gordon Perron (now deceased), Leonard and Arlyce Perron, Robert Patesel, Armando Gastaldo, Carol Hartley, Harold Leo Hennen Jr., Alice Binckley, George Martens, Jennings Morgan, Marge Thornton, George Monger, Michael Bower, and Robert Martin.

DEDICATION

This book is dedicated to everyone who may be seeking a way of life through a higher plane of learning, from the living Word of God.

To the person who is trying to reach for a better way of life and reverence for God.

To the person who may be searching for truth at any cost.

To the person who is not a Christian, this book is especially addressing itself to the truth concerning those things God has been waiting to tell you.

REVIEWER COMMENTS

Reverend Gary Sims — Ohio Director of Prison Fellowship, "You can do it brother Len." Without him, God would have had to assign someone else to encourage me and support my three years of hope in writing this book.

Margaret Beard — Educator, "The writing is clear and scholarly."

Robert Barclay — Educator, stressed keeping the message simple.

Andrew Sneller — England, my most pragmatic counselor.

Harry Hoover — Farmer, "Good for both non-Christians and Christians."

Walter J. Howdyshell — Lawyer, "I know this book will be a great help to any new child of God and a growth tool for anyone interested in God's Word."

W. O. Schoedinger — Entrepreneur, "Your book certainly has been good for me."

Virgil D. Mittelberg — Entrepreneur, "Easy to read and will help people grow spiritually."

J.R. McTammany — Pediatrician, "The depth of your conviction came through clearly and we were educated by your complete referencing."

Thomas J. Mills — Machinist, "You lead through God's Word, separating the points in an interesting way."

Charles Severance — Retired Grocer, "I love the book."

Harper Van Hoy — Farmer, "It very clearly answered most questions people have about the Bible and the plan of salvation."

Lillian Sears	Housewife, "Easy to understand."
Charles Lemly	Military, "Liked it all."
Pearl F. Daubenmire	"Easy to comprehend - Scriptural."
Gerald W. Miller	Metalsmith, "You touched all bases."
Harold Hennen	Gas company employee, "Gave a lot of answers I have looked for."
Regina Mecca	"... We know what God said." (Author's Sister)
Richard T. Taylor	Entrepreneur, liked best, "The intensity of the message."
Robert Patesel	Educator, "I'm pleased with your book."
Lucinda Maxwell	Housewife, "Answers to basic Scriptures."
Sally Price	Housewife, "In trying to reach those with little or no Bible training, the simpler the better."
Howard Prior	Engineer, "I commend you for writing the most comprehensive book on this subject that I have ever had the pleasure of reading."

PREFACE

The composition of this book is based upon the Holy Bible. Its purpose is to connect or involve the reader with the Holy Scriptures. Benefits include insight and knowledge from God's Word, which brings enlightenment, and new hope toward restoration with God.

Our behavior is affected by our values of right and wrong. Justice finds its balance through our laws. Laws, which are based upon God's Word, bring order and discipline. Discipline brings self-respect and fulfillment.

Purpose for living finds new dimension when we reach out to others. Happiness and peace of mind find their direction when we know where we are headed. When life is perceived as final the day we die, hope diminishes a little each passing day. Recognizing life as never ending is the hope of all who come to believe in Jesus Christ, who said; "Apart from me you can do nothing" (John 15:5). Apart from God's Word, we continue to grope for answers. This author believes in the Incarnate Lord Jesus Christ. The Word of God reveals His love through His Son. When man sets himself apart from God's Son, he sets himself apart from God. Reading with an open mind the content in this book may change your life. The author's words are intended to lead the reader to the most important words, the Words of God. They have the greatest authority. Reading and studying the Bible itself is far better than reading what someone else thinks about it.

The core matter of each chapter in this book is evangelical in nature and repetitious in character, which is common to the salvation message of God. Coming to know Jesus Christ in a personal way brings us to God. Through faithfulness and obedience to the Word of God, we grow in grace. Bible knowledge brings with it maturity. New relationships develop when we take time to study those things that God has prepared for us. This book is for everyone.

What Everyone Should Know About The Holy Bible attempts to unfold the freshness of a new birth, required by God. The overall worthiness of reading this book will be in direct proportion to the reader's personal dedication to learn. Why not learn more about the things that God has prepared for you? "Therefore consider carefully how you listen ...," said Jesus in Luke 8:18.

"WHAT EVERYONE SHOULD KNOW ABOUT THE HOLY BIBLE" has been prepared as a reverential study guide about the things of God. It is also an affirmation of the writer's faith in all that God has prepared for all people.

It is the author's hope that God will richly bless each and every person who will give a little time to reading this book. Coming to know the truth concerning the Holy Scriptures in this publication is the most important part of this presentation.

WORTH THINKING ABOUT

Through the Word, *we know* what God said.

Through God's love, *we find* His grace.

Through Christ, *we have* the Father and the Holy Spirit.

Through the Holy Spirit, *we have* the truth made known.

Through faith, *we have* salvation.

Through his forgiveness, *we have* restoration.

Through prayer, *we receive* answers.

Through behavior, *we find* tranquillity.

Through obedience, *we have* victory.

Through commitment, *we find* resolve.

Through love, *we overturn* hostility and conflict.

CHAPTER 1

THE HOLY BIBLE, THE WORD OF GOD

The Holy Bible is the inspired, unerring Word of God. It is God's distinct way of telling mankind who He is, who man is, why He created man, and what He expects. While it reveals God's love, it also gives notice of His wrath. It exposes the condition of man, good or evil. It provides a course of action for man to follow. Its doctrines are set apart, its record is binding, and its histories are true. The Holy Scriptures did not come by the will of man, but by holy men as they were moved by the Holy Spirit (2 Peter 1:20,21).

Until Jesus Christ returns for His believers, the Holy Spirit will guide believers into all truth (John 16:13). The Spirit is truth (1 John 5:6). New believers are established in truth and this truth is made known from the written word. The Bible is the basic and most important written record about God, and his love for humanity. Those who believe in the written Word and find their salvation will have an everlasting life with God (Reference James 1:21). The Bible is the greatest book ever written. God knew we would require His help in all areas of our lives. Anyone may come to these precious Words of God. They will find comfort in time of sorrow, and guidance in times of tribulation. Those who receive God's Word will by God's power come to know that it is not the words of men (1 Thessalonians 2:13).

The Bible is filled with many true happenings of early biblical times. As the Bible exposes man's immoral state, it also tells of God's plan to restore man to Him. The first book of the Bible, Genesis, reveals the first Messianic promise (Genesis 3:15). The last book of the Old Testament, (Malachi 3:1) (397 BC) tells of the coming of two messengers: John the Baptist and Jesus Christ. The Scribes and the Pharisees, even when facing Jesus did not connect this prophecy to the man standing before them.

The New Testament book of Matthew, chapter 1 verse 21, tells how that Mary would bear a son, which was Jesus Christ. The Old Testament book of Isaiah, chapter 53, tells of the sufferings of Christ. Again, this was over seven hundred years before Jesus Christ came. How much are you aware of these things and the effect they have on your life today? God's grace is for all who will believe his word.

The Bible reveals fundamental truths concerning God's laws and His love, which are found only through Jesus Christ. The Bible is the most important starting place for a man's religion. It offers the correct building blocks for spiritual growth. Through it is found wisdom, knowledge, and the fear of the Lord. There are many interpretations, but only one truth. Truth is truth, it is unchangeable, even as Christ is unchangeable and will not pass away with time (Mark 13:31). The Holy Bible is His word; it reveals His purpose and bears fruit when received in the heart of man. Isaiah 55:11 declares the Word as coming from the mouth of God Himself. "So is my word that goes out from my mouth: It will not return to me empty, but will accomplish what I desire and achieve the purpose for which I sent it."

Second Timothy 3:16 shows its true purpose. "All scripture is God breathed and is useful for teaching, rebuking, correcting and training in righteousness." Living according to God's Word brings great fruit in the lives of those who want to know the truth.

The next passage of Scripture has been called the master key to prayer. It may also be called "The Master's Key". Jesus gives us a great secret with only two conditions: living in Him, and allowing His Words to guide us. Listen to the Master: "If you remain in me and my words remain in you, ask whatever you wish, and it will be given you" (John 15:7).

The Scrolls, or the Holy Scriptures, were considered to be everything to "the religion" of the Israelites. The Sadducees and the Pharisees were in error and did not see what the Scriptures were telling them concerning the Messianic message. Jesus reprimanded them when he said, "You are in error because you do not know the Scriptures or the power of God" (Matthew 22:29).

TODAY'S ADVANTAGES

We are fortunate today to have both the Old and New Testaments. Studying them will add a new dimension to life. They unfold the will of God, which is salvation through Jesus Christ. Even with the advantages of today's concordances, bible commentaries, and computerized helps, it is important to understand the basic rules. Pray before you open this Holy Book, and ask God to allow His Holy Spirit to help you discover the truth concerning the specific area of the Bible you will be reading.

WHAT DOES GOD EXPECT FROM US?

He tells us to search the Scriptures (the word of God), because they tell us about eternal life (John 5:39). Romans 15:4 teaches that through endurance, we might have hope and this hope is in the Lord Jesus Christ. He expects all people to believe in his Son. "...Anyone who does not believe God has made him out to be a liar, because he has not believed the testimony God has given about his Son" (1 John 5:10). Too often people do not know what God expects from them because they fail to read the Holy Bible.

HIS WORD—LIKE SEED

The word bible means book. The Holy Bible contains God's word, or Seed. When planted, it will sprout into knowledge and wisdom. It will bring peace and joy unlike anything this world can give. When divine wisdom enters the heart, it is always followed by knowledge and is pleasant to the soul.

TRUTH IS MADE KNOWN ONLY BY THE HOLY SPIRIT

The Bible was not written through the intellectual mind of man. "For prophecy never had its origin in the will of man, but men spoke from God as they were carried along by the Holy Spirit" (2 Peter 1:21). We can study the writings of great philosophers with the natural mind, and by diligent application grasp their meaning, but the Word of God is different. The gift of the Holy Spirit, given to new believers, also carries them into the knowledge of the truth (Acts 2:38, 1 Timothy 2:4). Spiritual growth comes only through the power of the Holy Spirit when the Christian diligently studies and searches the Holy Bible. Coming to know the will of God requires a humble spirit, an attitude of sincerity, patience, and determination.

THE HOLY BIBLE—GIFT FROM ABOVE

This library of sixty-six books is reported to have been written by 35 different authors over a period of over some fifteen hundred years. The authors were from many different backgrounds—educated and

3

uneducated, including teachers, fisherman, farmers, kings and physicians. Subjects include poetry, biography, prophecy, law, history, and religion. Interestingly, many authors did not know one another yet the Bible is in absolute harmony. In 1546 AD the Roman Catholic Council of Trent declared eleven books known as the books of the Apocrypha to be canonical (by Church law) and included them in the Catholic edition of the Scriptures, however, they are not included in the Protestant Bible. The view of the Protestant Church is that while some of these books do contain material of literary merit and historical value, their canonicity has been rejected. The books of the apocrypha have been gradually omitted from Protestant Bibles for the following reasons: (1) they were never quoted by Jesus, (2) early scholars regarded them as uninspired, and (3) they did not appear in the ancient Hebrew cannon. (Source Thompson's Bible p. 179 KJV).

BIBLE LITERACY

If you are a Christian, where do you stand on bible literacy? Those who write about such things say, too many Christians do not know much about the Bible, yet the Bible is the foundation of their religion. *In the appendix, you will find a categorical listing of things often asked about.* If you would give a little time following up on these things which are listed, it will improve your knowledge about the Bible. You will learn about baptism, the church, Christian living, faith, fellowship and relationship with God, the Holy Spirit, our infallible God, Jesus Christ, judgment, law, obedience, paradise, prayer, promises, salvation, sin, truth, warnings, witnessing and worship. Learning to locate these things in the Bible will sharpen your interest and enrich your study. Why not give it everything you can to learn about these things which God has given us?

JESUS AND ISAIAH TELL ABOUT THE WORD OF GOD

This chapter addresses itself to the Book of Ages. Let us carefully consider what Jesus and Isaiah said about the Holy Bible. Jesus said, "The Spirit gives life; the flesh counts for nothing. The words [of scripture] I have spoken to you are spirit and they are life" (John 6:63). The Old Testament prophet Isaiah, in 760 BC. said, "The grass withers and the flowers fall, but the word of our God stands forever" (Isaiah 40:8). It is also very interesting to learn that Jesus, 790 years later, said a similar thing. "I tell you the truth, until heaven and earth disappear, not the smallest letter, not the least stroke of a pen, will by any means disappear from the Law until everything is accomplished" (Matthew 5:18).

Whatever your religious or denominational background, do not put off a study of the Bible. It is certain to bring spiritual maturity and peace. 1 Peter 2:2 tells us, "Like newborn babies, crave pure spiritual milk, so that by it you may grow up in your salvation." We see here God's plan. He asks all people to believe in His Son, and grow in grace and knowledge of the person of Jesus Christ.

KNOW WHO YOUR TEACHER IS!

In 1 John 2:27 God says, "As for you, the anointing you received from him remains in you, and you do not need anyone to teach you about all things and as that anointing is real, not counterfeit—just as it had taught you, remain in him." This does not mean we pay no attention to bible preachers or teachers. It does mean we are to pay attention to what is being said, so that, even as the Holy Spirit teaches us, we can know when unscriptural teachings occur. This is why it is important to read the Holy Bible daily and grow according in the written word. We should be very careful as we start to depend upon others to reveal the Word of God. Remember the Bible principle: God, through the Holy Spirit makes known the truth of Scriptures. The preacher, teacher, evangelist, elder, bishop, and pastor utilize their respective God given talents in presenting the Word of God and expounding upon it. The Holy Spirit makes known the truth to the one seeking Bible truth. All Biblical interpretations are not the same. This is one reason opinions about the Word of God vary.

WAYS OF BIBLE STUDY

There are many ways and means to study the Bible. Bible study classes at your local church, correspondence courses, listening to sermons, church school, or you can purchase a Bible study-aid book at your local Christian bookstore. However, beware of hesitation. When more than one way or means is offered, we tend to put things off. It may help you greatly if you would establish a general principle when using the Holy Scriptures for reading, studying, or meditating. Many people want to read through the entire Bible in one year. Bible reading calendars have been designed to do this. This is fine because it may help establish a deeper interest in the Bible.

Bible study may be enriched with the help of a concordance, or purchasing a Bible, which includes commentaries and annotations. Chain reference Bibles are a must when a deeper study is desired. Prayer and meditation are greatly enriched when the Scriptures are included in such activities.

This next suggestion may help you immensely. As you read and apply your mind to a deeper study, mark your bible with a symbol (s) to identify which passages are considered to be prophecy, God's promise, His command, or just a message from God. This will certainly enrich your study. The Bible should be taken literally because it is God's Word. Where symbolic, figurative language, a hyperbole (a figure of speech in which exaggeration is used for emphasis or effect), or parables, are used, keep an open mind toward the truth, which it represents. Above all remember the best rule, the Holy Spirit makes known the truth to the believer. "But the Counselor, the Holy Spirit, whom the Father will send in my name, will teach you all things and will remind you of everything I have said to you" (John 14:26). The Scriptures teach us that the Holy Spirit is our Helper on earth and Jesus is our Paraclete or Helper in heaven. Paraclete in Greek is "parakletos," and it means "one who speaks in favor of." Read John 14:16, John 15:26, John 16:7, John 16:13, and 1 John 2:1,2.

THE FIRST TIMER

Pray to God, ask for His guidance in your newfound commitment to study the Holy Bible. Use a King James Bible that includes a concordance. The NIV version used in this book allows for a meshing of writing style and ease of reading. The King James Version was written in 1611. It's been used for three hundred and eighty eight years. Study the Bible daily starting with the four Gospels. The book of Matthew references itself to the Jewish prophecies. Mark—shows Christ as the tireless Servant of God and man. The book of Luke purposes itself in a connected and orderly narrative of the life of Christ as seen by eye- witnesses. The book of John reveals the deity of Christ.

The book of John is a faith builder for those who want to come to know just who the Son of God really is. All other New Testament books will help you grow according to God's Word. If you are consistent in your efforts using this suggested manner of Bible study, you will have not only grown in the Word of God, but you will want to deepen your study of all the Holy Scriptures throughout your life in both the Old and New Testament. Many other aspects of your beliefs and convictions will be lifted

Reading and studying the Scriptures is not like picking up a fictional book and finding amusement. It differs greatly because you soon come to realize who the author is—God Himself. Remember that prayer preparation toward learning will bring you closer to understanding what it means to revere God. Some time ago I read about two men with no faith who started out to disprove the Holy Bible and ended up giving their lives to Christ. Without faith, the Bible is just a book as any other, but with faith, all things are possible. Hebrews 11:6 says, "And without faith it is impossible to please God, because anyone who comes to him must believe that he exists and he rewards those who earnestly seek him." When you begin to read and study the Holy Bible, you are really reaching for truth and you will find it. God will reward you when you persistently seek to learn from His precious Holy Book.

GOD'S PROMISE TO THOSE WHO SEEK TRUTH

God directs those who seek understanding and wisdom to "call out" to Him and He will answer. Proverbs 2:9 tells us, "Then you will understand what is right and just and fair—every good path." When man decides to trust and honor God, God will then honor the man who is seeking truth. The Bible makes known God's will for us. Yes, it is a personal encounter with truth and is rich and beautiful, unlike any other happening in our life.

In a Sunday school booklet, I read about a wise preacher who claimed that the Gospel functions in two ways: it comforts the disturbed, and it disturbs the comfortable.

Missionaries on furlough from foreign soil tell how people in

7

THE WORD OF GOD

Missionaries on furlough from foreign soil tell how people in countries across the world travel on foot many miles and sit on rough logs and stumps or on dirt floors to worship with the church and to hear the Word of God preached. They love singing and praying and are not in any way disturbed by long sermons. Perhaps we can take a lesson from all of this. God's Word is man's only hope, not only in learning things about God's laws and his salvation, but also the quality of these God-based values which we should be leaving behind us, for the future of our children.

ORIGIN AND GROWTH OF THE BIBLE

From the Original Manuscripts to the modern translations of today, we continue to focus in on God's Word. Purpose, is to come to know what God says. Some say, the ethics of the Bible are for God's people. The Sermon on the Mount is for those who follow Christ. The Holy Bible is for good, to them, who want to read and obey God's Word. The King James Bible was published in 1611. It is reported to have won wide acceptance to readers all over the world. The King James Version itself is not limited to or associated with a particular religion. It does not favor theological or ecclesiastical opinions.

Since, the Original Manuscripts, many translations have been published. To learn more about the deeper aspects of Bible Versions and Translations, the respective, historical, literary, textual, information sources, and the editing or revising process should be carefully considered. The KJV continues to be used by scholars who are aware of the many changes made in some of our modern translations. The author of the book you hold in your hand used the New International Version to provide harmony in writing style and ease of reading. His study Bible has always been the King James Version. Some modern versions are known to use pronouns in place of nouns. Some have eliminated words and certain verses. Please consider this book as a study book for the Bible itself. Prayerfully take time to read both, above and below the referral passages used in this book. And remember what Jesus said, "Howbeit, when he, the Spirit of truth, is come, he will guide you into all truth..." (John 16:13 KJV). From this, we know that believers should expect the Holy Spirit to help them, to come into the knowledge of the truth. To His honor and Glory.

8

CHAPTER 2

GOD HIMSELF

Man has not seen God. God however has allowed us to see Himself in Christ Jesus. Paul told the Colossians that Jesus is God. He says, "He is the image of the invisible God..." (Colossians 1:15).

The Word of God is clear as Paul chants his praise to the immortal, invisible, and only wise God (1 Timothy 1:17). Jesus tells us, "No one has seen the Father except the one who is from God; only he [Jesus] has seen the Father" (John 6:46).

Are you looking for God? Man cannot have God without first coming to Jesus Christ, who himself said; "...No one comes to the Father except through me" (John 14:6). Jesus further tells us that He and the Father are one (John 10:30). What does this mean? This is the mystery of our faith in the Godhead of the Father, the Son, and the Holy Spirit. Belief in the Trinity is not the result of intellectual assent, but truth made known by God the Holy Spirit.

Jesus tells who He is. "I am the Alpha and the Omega, says the Lord God, who is, and who was, and who is to come, the Almighty" (Revelation 1:8). If not now, you may one day try to find God. People in every country seek to have God in their lives. Unfortunate are those who have been misled into thinking He will accept their fabricated bibles and doctrines. True, our God is the God of salvation. He has a specific plan that must be followed to establish hope of spiritual rescue from sin and death. Death here refers to a separation from God.

REMEMBERING GOD'S GREATEST
COMMANDMENT TO ALL MEN

The greatest commandment we have from God is to love Him with all of our heart, soul, and mind. The problem is, man keeps thinking being good and praying is his response to that commandment. To love God means to follow His commandments in a specific way (John 14:23).

THE ALMIGHTY POWER OF GOD

The "Great Power of God" in the first chapter of Genesis tells us the truth about heaven and earth— God created them. Many believe differently. Have you ever wondered why God created the heaven and the earth? I'm sure the skeptics of this world have their definitions and theories, but this writer will try to make two points. *First*, man cannot make even one spoon of dirt, simply because it has already been made. *Secondly*, the mysteries of God's creation of earth and heavenly bodies and their purpose have not been fully made known to man.

Man has attained certain knowledge concerning the universe. *Its effects, depiction, distances, energies, formations, dimensions, physics and relationships, have been under study, but true divine PURPOSE has not been uncovered.* Cosmological theories about the universe have been under study for many centuries. Einstein was convinced that the cosmos is an orderly, continuous unity (time). We know that God did create heaven and earth. The first opening words in Genesis say, "In the beginning God created the heavens and the earth." The Hebrew language uses the word "bara", which means create. Its phonetic application demands a rolling of the letter "R". As you pronounce it to yourself, keep in mind that in Hebrew, the word "bara" clearly means only God can "bara", or create. God is not only creator, He is also all authority of the heavens and the earth. God keeps all things through His own power.

The power, authority, knowledge, and the wisdom of God are awesome. Nehemiah 9:6 tells us, "You alone are the Lord. You made the heavens, even the highest heavens, and all their starry host, the earth and all that is on it, the seas and all that is in them. You give life to everything, and the multitudes of heaven worship you."

God created all things through Jesus Christ (Ephesians 3:9). When Christ was on the earth two thousand years ago He said, "before Abraham was born, I am" (John 8:58). Here we begin to see the oneness of God and Jesus Christ. He was God in the flesh.

10

JOHN TELLS ABOUT THE DEITY OF CHRIST

Let us compare these next two passages from John 1:1 and 14. *Verse 1,* "In the beginning was the Word, and the Word was with God, and the Word was God." *Verse 14 says,* "The Word became flesh and made his dwelling among us. We have seen his glory, the glory of the One and only, who came from the Father, full of grace and truth."

John's detailed account is to show that God and His Word, who is Christ, are one and the same. The Word with a capital "W" is referenced to Jesus Christ. The word used with a small "w" is associated with "the word of God." Example of this is in this next passage from Psalms 33:6, "By the word of the Lord were the heavens made..."

From this, we learn the following. "The Word became flesh" refers to Christ Himself, and through His Incarnation, God came into our midst. Important also is what the Apostle John said, in 1 John 4:2,3. "This is how you can recognize the *Spirit of God*: Every spirit that acknowledges that Jesus Christ has come in the flesh is from God, but every spirit that does not acknowledge Jesus is not from God. This is the spirit of the Antichrist, which you have heard is coming and even now is already in the world."

THE AWESOME POWER OF GOD

It is by the breath of our mouth that our words come, and by the breath of God's mouth came creation. David praised God when he said, in 1 Chronicles 29:12, "Wealth and honor come from you; you are the ruler of all things. In your hands are strength and power to exalt and give strength to all."

FIRST REVEALING OF GOD'S NAME

Exodus 3:14 records God saying, "I AM WHO I AM." God is infinite, without boundaries or limits. With Him there is no beginning or ending. He exists by His own power and might.

JESUS REVEALS WHO HE IS

"I tell you the truth," Jesus answered, "before Abraham was born, I am!" (John 8:58). We continue to disclose here in this chapter on GOD HIMSELF that Jesus and God are one.

THE CHARACTER OF GOD

God is the creator and sustainer of the universe. His revelations, judgments, attributes, characteristics, love, and incarnate manifestations are recorded in the Holy Bible. This is great, right... but all of this means nothing unless you believe. Those who do not believe forfeit a great truth. God is love and His greatest creation is man. He made man in His own image. We may take this to mean we have the capacity to live by the law of love. *The law of love is forgiveness.* We also have the capacity for patience, kindness, forgiveness, and faithfulness to God. Other living things do not.

Adam and Eve, because of their disobedience to God, lost their place in paradise. Their faithfulness to God stopped when they sinned. The recorded historical events concerning man's depravity or immorality caused God to reveal His anger many times. The Old Testament repeatedly tells of God's reaction to the ungodliness of man's sinful behavior. God cannot and will not put up with sin. God warns man to choose a way of life, which is right and correct with Him. He continues to be patient with each one of us.

Man was made for God. Why? To bring Him glory. God, though, was sorry that He made man. If it were not for Noah, man might not have occupied this earth for very long. All through history, man has demonstrated his stubbornness to the laws of God. God is faithful, forbearing, patient, long-suffering, gentle, covenant keeping, self-revealing, prayer hearing, virtue-loving, giving, and forgiving. Is this your God? He certainly is my God. This is the God I want to praise continually. We should not fool with His wrath or anger. His judgments are fierce, and He knows the heart of every man, woman, and child.

12

ABOUT GOD'S LOVE BEFORE AND AFTER SALVATION

This question was asked in a Sunday school class regarding God's love: If *you don't accept salvation, do you have God's love?* The Bible is our source for the answer to this question. 1 John 4:16 tells us, "God is love." He is not about love, He is love. God does not turn His love on and off. *His love is never ending.* He wants all to be saved and he is waiting upon His believers to convey the Good News of Christ. God loves everyone and wants everyone to be in union with Him, but it is sin, which separates us from the love of God.

This next verse of Scripture tells us everything we should know concerning God's love through Christ's atoning sacrifice for our sins. It means that by His life, death, and resurrection, He has won us the favor of God. "This is love: not that we loved God, but that he loved us and sent his Son as an atoning sacrifice for our sins" (1 John 4:10).

KNOWS ALL, SEES ALL, AND HEARS ALL

God is Omnipotent!   He has absolute power and authority.

God is Omnipresent!   He is everywhere.

God is omniscience!   He knows everything.

God is not a respecter of persons!   This means that He is not interested in our placing any agenda above His, and He does not show favoritism. (Acts 10:34). He knows the needs of everyone, even before they ask. God calls his people and He delivers them from doom. He gives certain gifts or talents to everyone.

God is sovereign! He is supreme in power and authority. Man can add nothing to whatever has been made by God. God has already made everything that has been made. The full revelation and love of God is in Jesus Christ. Man's only hope of coming close to understanding the mind of God is through the Holy Bible and God's Spirit. The limitations of the human mind keep man from understanding the deep mysteries of God. God is Spirit, changeless, all-powerful, all-knowing, righteous, holy, and eternal.

ONLY WAY TO GOD IS THROUGH JESUS CHRIST

If you have some inclination toward Jesus Christ but do not believe you are worthy, or that he is not for real, then may I say this to you? Open your heart to the door of life; listen to what Jesus has already said to those who would come to trust Him as their personal Savior. "Here I am! I [Jesus] stand at the door, and knock. If anyone hears my voice, and opens the door, I will come in and eat with him, and he with me" (Revelation 3:20). What is your motivating force today? Is it riches, fame, religion, position, or just nothing at all? Many have come to realize they need Christ as their Savior. Do, give it some thought.

Jesus is standing at the door right this very moment, and if you have not really and truly invited Him into your heart, won't you do so right now? This book was written with the express purpose of showing God's love for you. The scriptures included here are for real and for you. The writer of this book would like to show you how you can come into His presence, His Word, His love, and His Son. Your personal Savior is waiting in the wings ready to accept you, whatever you may think about your life or your sins. God has made provisions for you and your family. God loves you and wants you to come to know him in a personal way. He has shown Himself in Christ. Jesus is the visible person of the invisible God. The character of God is love, not hate. He has one desire, one will for man—salvation through Jesus Christ. Are you apart from God?

Do you have a true relationship with Him? Why not take seriously the many promises of the Bible? If you are right in this decision, you have everything to gain.

"Be still, and know that I am God; I will be exalted among the nations, I will be exalted in the earth" (Psalms 46:10).

CHAPTER 3

JESUS CHRIST, SON OF THE LIVING GOD

Jesus Christ came into this world both human and divine. God's Holy Word tells of His dual nature. "He appeared in a body, was vindicated by the Spirit, was seen by angels, was preached among the nations, was believed on in the world, was taken up in glory" (1 Timothy 3:16). Jesus came to fulfill the will of the Father, "who wants all men to be saved and come to the knowledge of the truth" (1 Timothy 2:4)

When Jesus was baptized in the Jordan River, God announced His pleasure in His Son. "And a voice from heaven said, this is my Son, whom I love; with him I am well pleased" (Matthew 3:17). Jesus is the Son of the Living God, who came into the world to make possible a means for man's recovery from a hell-destined excursion. If man does not come into accord with God's plan for atonement, he will perish. Jesus said, in Luke 13:3, "But unless you repent, you too will all perish."

The world is filled with religions of all kinds. *Christianity is solely based upon the Son of the Living God, Jesus Christ.* If you have not yet done so then why not become a student of the New Testament and study the life of Christ. The book of John tells of His deity. Come to know His many teachings, His many miracles, how He healed the sick, forgave men of their sins, and showed compassion to countless numbers. Learn about His life, His upbringing, and His ministry. *Coming to know Him is to come to know God, because they are one.* You will learn who Jesus Christ is, and His significance to God's eternal plan for you and your loved ones.

Jesus Christ is the only means to have a right relationship with the Jehovah God of the Bible. Jesus is our high priest according to Hebrews 4:14, "Therefore, since we have a great high priest who has gone through the heavens, Jesus the Son of God, let us *hold firmly* to the faith we profess." *Everything has been done for us at the cross of Christ.* It is now up to us to preserve and testify with respect, to His

15

finished work. Jesus Christ is the only one who can take away sin (John 1:29). His agonizing suffering and death was His own voluntary sacrifice. He said that no one took His life; He laid it down.

The whole world should be jumping up and down, shouting praises, clapping their hands, singing songs of great joy and adoration, for the greatest champion and hero of all time, Jesus Christ. Instead, the people of the world give Him little or no credit for the greatest act of love ever given to humanity. People in Jesus' time were blind to these things and many in this day see no better.

Why is it that Jesus is not acknowledged publicly by the great world leaders of this day? Jesus obviously knew the ignorance of all men and had asked His disciples this question. "Who do you say I am?" Simon Peter answered, "You are the Christ, the Son of the living God" (Matthew 16:16). Are people afraid they will be called religious when they acknowledge the Savior of the world? Those who testify of Christ are doing what He has asked.

Who do you think Jesus Christ is? What does He really mean to you? He is a true friend to many people. Some hold Him as the Lord of their lives; some know Him as Peter did, "Son of the Living God." This view, though, is not shared by all. Some regard Jesus as nothing more than a figure in history. Many believe he was just a teacher. Even in His time, in His own town, they jeered Him by saying, "He's only the son of a carpenter." Some use the name of Jesus to further their fabricated religions. Some laugh and scoff at the very name of Jesus, and some are called "Jesus lovers." Some, through ignorance, become irritated when His name is mentioned. *His coming was announced in the 8th Century BC.* The most preeminent prophet, Isaiah, recorded in Isaiah 7:14, "Therefore, the Lord himself shall give you a sign: The virgin will be with child, will give birth to a son, and will call him Emmanuel." This virgin turned out to be Mary, the mother of Jesus. The religious leaders of that day disregarded the Scriptural prophecy about the coming of Christ. Jesus was with them and they did not know Him (John 1:26). Most people today don't know Christ, and many just ignore Christ.

HIS MINISTRY BEGAN AT THE AGE OF THIRTY

Now grown at the age of thirty and being with His disciples, Jesus said He would be delivered up before the gentiles. He said He would be mocked and spat upon spitefully and put to death. He said He would rise on the third day. (Luke 18:31,32). The disciples did not understand what He was saying (vs.34). Today, we, the people of this 20th century, have a greater advantage. The news of Jesus Christ has been preached in all parts of the world (Colossians 1:23). The Holy Bible is available everywhere. The world is without excuse. How about you? Have you ever really and truly acknowledged Jesus Christ as your personal Savior? *Many people know the historical Christ, but never come to know the personal Christ.* If you are a believer in Him already, then it is good to know that He prayed for all of His future believers. Here's what He said: "My prayer is not for them alone [meaning the disciples], I pray also for those [future believers] who will believe in me through their message" (John 17:20). [King James reads "their word"]. The "message" or word, which Jesus uses here, is the message of our witness about Christ, specifically; that He was sent from God the Father and through Him anyone can be saved.

COMING TO KNOW GOD THROUGH JESUS CHRIST

Recorded in the Holy Scriptures are the "I AM's" of Christ. The "I AM's" of Christ, recorded in the Books of John and Revelation, reveal a broad register of who He is. In Exodus 3:14 God says to Moses, "I am that I am." Some four thousand years later Jesus said, "Before Abraham was born, I am!" (John 8:58). This is no coincidence. We see here the oneness of God the Father and Christ Jesus.

THE "I AM's" OF CHRIST
(Jehovah or Yahweh means, "I am")

The Messiah	John 4:26
The Bread of Life	John 6:35
From Above	John 8:23
The Eternal One	John 8:58

17

The Light of The World	John 9:5
The Door (KJV)	John 10:7
The Son of God	John 10:36
The Resurrection and Life	John 11:25
Lord and Master (KJV)	John 13:13
The Way, Truth and Life	John 14:6
The True Vine	John 15:1
Alpha and Omega	Revelation 1:8
The First and the Last	Revelation 1:17

THE DIVINITY OF CHRIST

Jesus said in Revelation 1:8, "I am the Alpha and Omega," says the Lord God, "who is, and who was, and who is to come, the almighty." Now cross-reference this verse with what God said to Moses in Exodus 3:14 "I AM WHO I AM".

Are we telling our children this today? The divinity of Jesus Christ is well established in the New Testament.

He claimed to be God in that He was with the Father before creation (John 17:5).

He is called God by God the Father (Hebrews 1:8).

He is called God by the apostle Thomas (John 20:28).

He claimed to be God in that He was before Abraham (John 8:58).

He forgives sin; only God can forgive sin (Read Mark 2:5-11).

"THE SON IS THE RADIANCE OF GOD'S GLORY"
(Hebrews 1:3)

Jesus Christ is the keeper of all things, "Sustaining all things by his powerful word" (Hebrews 1:3). Jesus said that he has been given

18

all power in heaven and earth (Matthew 28:18). Check it out as you study the Holy Bible; read it to be sure. God's own manifestation or presence in Jesus is truly something hard to understand and it is awesome. When God sees anyone making a vigorous search for truth and enlightenment, He will begin to fill them with knowledge and wisdom. Understanding will come and discretion will preserve and protect the seeker. Read Proverbs 2:1-11.

THE PRE-EXISTENT CHRIST

"Jesus Christ the same yesterday and today and forever" (Hebrews 13:8). He is faultless and complete. Nothing stays the same except Jesus Christ. This is why our eyes should never be taken off of Him.

The endlessness of Christ is revealed in these next passages. "Without father or mother, without genealogy, without beginning of days or end of life, like the Son of God he remains a priest forever" (Hebrews 7:3).

"And now, Father, glorify me in your presence with the glory I had with you before the world began" (John 17:5).

PROPHECY Messianic	FULFILLMENT
"And I will put enmity [hatred] between you [Satan] and the woman, and between your offspring and hers; he will crush your [Satan's] head, and you will strike his heel" [trials of Christ while on earth] (Genesis 3:15).	"But when the fullness of time was come, God sent forth His Son, made of a woman, [Mary] made under the law" (Galatians 4:4). Believers are resurrected with Christ (Romans 6:5).
"The days are coming," declares the Lord, "when I will raise up to David a righteous Branch [Jesus], and a King who will reign	"All authority in heaven and on earth has been given to me [Jesus]" (Matthew 28:18).

19

wisely and do what is just
and right in the land"
(Jeremiah 23:5).

"See I will send my
messenger [John the
Baptist], who will
prepare the way before
me [Jesus]. Then suddenly
the Lord you are seeking
will come to his temple;
the messenger of the
covenant [Jesus], whom
you desire, will come,"
says the Lord Almighty
(Malachi 3:1).

"And you my child, will be called
prophet of the most high [John
the Baptist]; for you will go on
before the Lord to prepare the
way for him, to give his people
the knowledge of salvation
through the forgiveness of their
sins." (Luke 1:76,77).

BIBLE PROPHECIES POINT TO CHRIST

Jesus is God's only means to regain possession of all souls. Isaiah 53:5 reads, "... and by His wounds we are healed." He is God's only answer to our redemption. He is the only way we can get into God's own righteousness. God loves what He has made, although He said in the time of Noah that he was sorry He made man. God has had many, many disappointments in man. Sending His only Son to redeem man from his sins is God's final covenant.

WE ARE MADE FOR GOD

Why did Jesus come to pay the penalty for our sins? It is very difficult to understand the deep mysteries of God. We must learn that God did not make us for ourselves, He made us for Him. Proverbs 16:4 says, "The Lord works out everything for his own ends—even the wicked for a day of disaster." We are made to serve God. We can, in a small way, compare God's love to the undying love of a normal mother filled with affection for her own children.

THE POWER OF CHRIST

The Pardoning of Sins: Matthew 9:6 tells us about the power of Christ when He was here upon this earth."... But so that you may know that the Son of man has the authority on earth to forgive sins..."

His Infinite Power: "All authority in heaven and on earth has been given to me" (Matthew 28:18).

His Power over Nature: "... He commands even the winds and the water, and they obey him..." (Luke 8:25).

Over His Own Life: "No one takes it from me, but I lay it down of my own accord..." (John 10:18).

Life Giving: "For you granted him authority over all people that he might give eternal life to all those you have given him" (John 17:2).

Working Wonders: "How God anointed Jesus of Nazareth with the Holy Spirit and power, and how he went around doing good and healing all who were under the power of the devil, because God was with him" (Acts 10:38).

HIS GRACE REIGNS

God's grace reigns through Jesus Christ. His grace reigns through righteousness forever (Romans 5:21). Because His grace reigns, it is the duty of the believer to live a life worth living, as God would want it. (Ephesians 6:14). Noah became heir of God's righteousness by faith (Hebrews 11:7). "...Everyone who does what is right has been born of Him" (1 John 2:29).

DISTINCTION OF A CHRIST-LIKE PERSON

There is nothing worth doing, or nothing worth thinking, unless it is fitting with God. He is always pleased with those who follow His commandments. "No one who is born of God will continue to sin, because God's seed remains in him; He cannot go on sinning, because he has been born of God" (1 John 3:9). *This verse has troubled many.* A deeper study shows us how Christ continues to mediate for Christians (1John 2:1,2). Remember, He said He would send us a Helper (John 14:26). Anyone who is "born of God" receives the gift of the Holy Spirit (Acts 2:38). He then helps believers to live according to their new life in Christ. As each day unfolds, the true follower of Christ should begin to act more like Christ. How? By following His teachings given in the Scriptures, and allowing the Holy Spirit, through faith, to lead a new life. *When sin does occur, and is confessed, Jesus intercedes for the believer with God. The cross paid the price and Christ continues in our behalf with God. Apart from Christ, we can do nothing (John 15:5).* Conversely, the believer can do everything through Christ (Philippians 4:13). The Bible is ever revealing the love of God through His Son. Most people of the world keep on ignoring the message and the Grace of God.

IMPORTANT THINGS TO KNOW ABOUT JESUS CHRIST
The Pre-existent Christ

Eternally the same	Hebrews 13:8
With no beginning	Hebrews 7:3
His activities eternal	Micah 5:2
Was before the creation of the world	John 1:1,17:5
Was before Abraham	John 8:58

The Messiah

Prophecy of His coming (607 BC)	Daniel 9:25
His sufferings, Satan's defeat	Genesis 3:15
His obscurity	Luke 2:51
His crucifixion	John 19: 18,24
His burial	John 19: 39-42
His resurrection	Matthew 28:6,7
His ascension	Mark 16: 19,20
His return	Acts 1:11

DISCIPLES ASKED FOR A SIGN OF HIS RETURN
The disciples asked Jesus when He would return to earth, and

22

when the world would come to an end (Matthew 24:3). Jesus responded by telling them not to look for signs. He also said, "Watch out that no one deceives you. For many will come in my name, claiming, "I am the Christ and will deceive many" (Matthew 24:4). The Scriptures do not reveal the time of Christ's Second Coming. Jesus said only the Father knows. Preparation for His return is very important. His returning referred to in Revelation 19:5-10 is called the wedding feast of the Lamb. It announces the wedding of the Lamb. This will be the time when Christ will return for His believers and followers, known as, the Church. Jesus said in John 14:3, "... I will come back and take you with me that you also may be where I am."

WEDDING OF THE LAMB

Christians should know what God expects from them. He inspires them through His written Word to help make them ready for the return of Christ through trusting, obeying, and following the teachings of His Son. Then the Church will be ready for Christ's return. "Let us rejoice and be glad and give him glory! For the wedding of the Lamb has come and his bride has made herself ready. Fine linen, bright and clean was given her to wear." Fine linen refers to the righteous acts of the saints. The spiritual readiness of the Church, through the indwelling of the Holy Spirit, will make her ready for that single most important day we are all waiting for, which is, Christ's return.

JESUS HAS ALREADY ASKED US TO BE READY FOR HIS COMING

Careful study of what happened in Noah's day may give us insight and help us to understand God's expectations and what it is we must do to be ready for Christ's coming. God called Noah to do a strange thing. He was to build a huge boat. Then, at a specific time he would place his family and certain animals and birds into the boat. God told Noah that He would flood the earth, and that all would perish except Noah, his family, and the birds and animals.

God saw the wickedness and evils of man which brought down His anger, as the earth was corrupt and filled with violence. The great flood came and all perished except those who were in the boat (see

Genesis 7:22,23). God's justice was served. He said never again would He flood the earth. The rainbow that we see today is evidence of God's promise (Read Genesis 9:8-17).

Christ's second coming will be followed by God's judgment as sure as the great flood, so, let's not consider this any more strange than what God told Noah. To the unbeliever all these things are strange. Appropriate preparation is vital. Jesus said, "... So you must be ready" (Matthew 24:44). What preparation have you made for the coming of the Son of Man? He is not asking us to build a boat, but He is asking us to prepare and be ready for His coming. This preparation is made through accepting Christ as our Savior, and then living a clean life as required by God.

"For in the days before the flood, people were eating and drinking, marrying and giving in marriage, up to the day Noah entered the ark; and they knew nothing about what would happen until the flood came and took them all away. That is how it will be at the coming of the Son of Man" (Matthew 24:38,39). What importance have you placed upon these things? Are you ready?

GOD IS STILL CALLING

Today there are all sorts of wickedness and violence in the world. God's call is the same today. He is calling everyone, but still most refuse to heed His calling. *Christ's Church is our spiritual life-boat.* To come into His Church, which is His Body requires the same faith that Noah had. What is your position on the subject of salvation through Jesus Christ? These Bible events concerning the great flood represent the faith of Noah and his family. They show how the mercy of God saved Noah and his family. God's mercy today is shown in the person of Christ Jesus.

THE COMMITMENT OF CHRIST

Jesus was committed to fulfill the will of the Father concerning His suffering and death, which is, and was, the only true atonement for the sins of humankind. I am ever so deeply moved when I read this next passage. "About the ninth hour Jesus cried out with a loud voice, saying, Eloi, lama sabachthani? Which means, My God My God, why have you forsaken me?" (Matthew 27:46).

Here is what Jesus went through for you and me. When He was upon the cross, He had a spiritual separation the moment He took our sins upon Himself. This was the hour, which He dreaded. He knew beforehand the indescribable suffering He would face. When Jesus took the sins of the world upon Himself in His final moments of suffering for our sake, He would shortly separate Himself from the Father. Two deaths occurred here: one was a spiritual separation and the other a physical separation. He knew in advance not only the physical pain that He would go through, but also more importantly what He was about to face—a spiritual separation from the Father.

OLD AND NEW TESTAMENT HARMONIC PASSAGES

Knowing very clearly that He would suffer, Jesus remained faithful and obedient. He prayed, "My Father, if it is possible, may this cup be taken from me. Yet not as I will, but as you will" (Matthew 26:39). *Then, on the third day, the hope of all future believers was born the hope of eternal life.* David expressed similar faithfulness and obedience when he said: "I have set the Lord always before me. Because he is at my right hand, I will not be shaken. Therefore my heart is glad and my tongue rejoices; my body will also rest secure, because you will not abandon me to the grave, nor will you let your Holy One see decay" (David's record is in Psalms 16:8-10). David knew the will of God in his life. Have you come to know the will of God for your life?

HOW DOES ANYONE BECOME A CHRISTIAN?

Romans 10: 9-10 gives a most meaningful message to those who will read and listen. It says: *"That if you confess with your mouth, Jesus is Lord, and believe in your heart that God raised him from the dead, you will be saved. For it is with your heart that you believe and are justified, and it is with your mouth that you confess and are saved."* Please notice very carefully; it is not religion that saves a person, it is faith in Jesus Christ, a verbal admission, and a personal commitment to turn away from sinning.

About the resurrection! Jesus said "... because I live, you also will live" (John 14:19). The Church does not save; it is only through the person of Jesus Christ that one is saved. The Church is the collective members of His Body. To think or practice otherwise is to embrace the doctrines of men. Let no one fool you with doctrine, which is contrary to the written Word of God.

WILL YOU BE READY?

The believer, whether he is physically alive or has already passed from this life, will be with Christ at His Second Coming. Are you prepared for the day when Jesus will return for His Believers? His coming will be swift and sudden. There will be no opportunity to play catch up, last minute repentance, or compromise. When Christ comes for His body of believers, everything will have been made ready, according to God's plan and timing. It is written in the Bible. The single most important decision anyone can make in his entire life is the decision to call upon the name of Jesus Christ.

Are you prepared? Noah listened to God. Remember that it is not through any religious ceremonies that we are made right with God. It is simply through listening to the call of Christ, which is written, and then making a firm commitment to trust, follow and obey all that is written in the Holy Scriptures.

WHAT DOES THE BIBLE MEAN, "TO OVERCOME"?

It is only when we realize and believe this next passage that we overcome. "For all have sinned and fall short of the glory of God, and are justified freely by his grace through the redemption that came by Jesus Christ" (Romans 3: 23,24). Yes, it is true; we overcome by listening, repenting, and calling upon the name above all names, Jesus Christ.

Those who follow His teaching can agree on the following: God's love is for all people and is shown through Jesus Christ, the Son of the Living God. The Bible reveals God's mercy and grace. The message in First John 2:12,14, (to those who overcame), is clear and is applicable to all people of this day. He addressed his message to "children and fathers," who were mature in their faith, and the younger men who

26

had won the victory through Christ. He said, "and *you have overcome* the evil one." John also tells why the young men had overcome. He said, "... I write to you, young men, because you are strong, and *the Word of God lives in you...*" (1 John 2:14). Believers grow stronger when they study the Word of God, and then live according to it.

FROM THE MASTER HIMSELF

Jesus gives us a vital message in Revelation 2: 7. He says, "He who has an ear, let him hear what the Spirit says to the churches. *To him who overcomes,* I will give the right to eat from the tree of life, which is in the paradise of God."

Readiness comes through submission to Christ and obedience to the written Word. Think of it this way. God has given us everything we need to prepare ourselves for His coming. *Through His Son we have life* (1 John 5:11). *Through His Word we have truth* (John 17:17). *Through His Spirit we have His guarantee of everlasting life* (Ephesians 4:30). What a mighty God we serve!

WHO BELIEVES IN THE DOCTRINE OF JESUS CHRIST?

Answer —not the vast majority of the population of this earth. It's almost no different today than in Jesus' day when He was preaching in His own hometown of Nazareth. He was questioned as to His credentials and they said, "Isn't this the carpenter's son? Isn't his mother's name Mary? And aren't his brothers James, Joseph, Simon and Judas?" (Matthew 13:53-58). Their words were negative without respect.

Jesus knew there was no respect for Him in His own town. Today, the disciples of the Lord find it no different. Certainly, there are people who come into a saving faith in Jesus Christ today. However, as we look at the population as a whole, only a few are listening to the salvation message, and only few are giving it. Today we have more religions that are not Christian than ever before. Religion is on the rise, not salvation, or baptism. Our witnessing about Christ can change this.

CHRIST—HEART OF THE CHRISTIAN'S RELIGION

The heart of the believer is centered in Jesus Christ. Without the

27

doctrine of Jesus Christ there is no true church, no true faith, and no true belief. Paul said we are to teach no other doctrine (1 Timothy 1:3). The doctrine of Christ is what Jesus taught and what He accomplished in His birth, death, and resurrection. The apostle John said, "Anyone who runs ahead and does not continue in the teaching of Christ does not have God; whoever continues in the teaching has both the Father and the Son" (2 John verse 9). John further said, ""If anyone comes to you and does not bring this teaching, do not take him into your house or welcome him. Anyone who welcomes him shares in his wicked work" (2 John verses 10-11).

To know Jesus is to know how He thinks.

To be like Jesus is to do as He would do.

To make Jesus your Lord is to do what He commands.

When we find out what His laws are, we find out how He thinks. When we follow His laws, we become like Him, and please God. When we make Him our Lord, He then becomes our Lord. Obedience to His Word will bring confidence in our walk. To "overcome" requires obedience. Believing and applying diligent effort to follow Christ will bring many great rewards. Jesus said, "Blessed are those who wash their robes [live up to God's commandments], that they may have the right to the tree of life and may go through the gates into the city" (Revelation 22:14).

The greatest power in the universe is God. Simply put, God is God. His love for all of mankind is expressed through His only Son, who came to this earth as a "Lamb". The Lamb, Christ, was and remains, the only perfect sacrifice ever required by God to reconcile believers to Himself (John 1:29). His one time sacrifice was completed at the cross. His final words were "It is finished" (John 19:30). It requires no additive or substitutions. The true Christian should not take his eyes off Christ Jesus because "He truly is the way, the truth, and the life " (John 14:6).

ONE SACRIFICE....IS ALL THAT GOD REQUIRED

"But when this priest (Jesus Christ) had offered for all time one sacrifice for sins, he sat down at the right hand of God" (Hebrews 10:12). "Because by one sacrifice he (Jesus) has made perfect forever those who are being made holy" (Hebrews 10:14).

Jesus is the Christ (Savior) of the bible. He is the One who was baptized by John the Baptist and was the One to whom God said, "This is my Son, whom I love; with him I am well pleased" (Matthew 3:17).

If God said He is well pleased, then how about you? Have you truly received Him into your heart as your Savior? Are you well pleased with Jesus Christ? "Yet to all who received him, to those who believed in his name, he gave the right to become children of God, children not born of natural descent, nor of human decision or a husband's will, but born of God" (John 1:12,13).

"I tell you the truth, he who believes has everlasting life" (John 6:47). These words of Christ literally say, you have my word on it... signed, *Jesus Christ*. Who is Christ? He is God who came in the form of man so that we could recognize Him. Believe it to be sure.

To the Samaritan woman at the water well, Jesus, said; "If you knew the gift of God and who it is that asks you for a drink, you would have asked him and he would have given you living water" (vs 10). She questioned Jesus as to where he would get this living water. He said, "Everyone who drinks this water will be thirsty again, but whoever drinks the water I give him will become in him a spring of living water welling up to eternal live" (vs 13). The woman said, "I know that Messiah (called Christ) is coming. When he comes, he will explain everything to us. Then Jesus declared, *I who speak to you am he* [the Messiah]" (verses 25,26). Do, read the whole accounting in John 4: 4-26. Christ is the answer to this weary world deeply in need of a Savior. He certainly was the answer for me and for all who call upon his name. Jesus said, "All that the Father gives me will come to me, and whoever comes to me I will never drive away (John 6:37).

" CHRIST IS THE ANSWER "

CHAPTER 4

THE HOLY SPIRIT

The Holy Spirit is the third person of the Divine Trinity. The Holy Spirit is equal with the Father and the Son. The Holy Spirit is a person. We must never speak of Him as "it," or think of Him as only an influence, as it degrades God Himself. He is God the Holy Spirit in the same way that Jesus was God manifested in the flesh and is the Son. The Holy Bible reveals the Father, the Son, and the Holy Spirit as one in the same Godhead.

The word "trinity" is not found in the Bible. The Trinity is expressed by Jesus who said, "Therefore go and make disciples of all nations, baptizing them in the name of the Father, and of the Son and of the Holy Spirit" (Matthew 28:19). The Holy Trinity is not something we can understand in physiological terms because it is spiritual. Paul writes in Romans 11:33, "Oh, the depth of the riches of the wisdom and knowledge of God! How unsearchable his judgments, and his paths beyond tracing out!" The doctrine of the Trinity (three distinct persons in One God-Head), has confounded many people throughout time. The Word of God reveals the Father, the Son, and the Holy Ghost. The heart of Christendom is— Father, Son, and Holy Ghost.

Trusting in Jesus Christ brings peace and confidence in what God has provided for those wanting to learn and grow. Anyone who will take the time and have the right intention can learn about the God of all creation and the Son of God and the Holy Spirit.

Let us review what Jesus said to the disciples just before He ascended to heaven: "But the Counselor, the Holy Spirit, whom the Father will send in my name, will teach you all things and remind you of everything I have said to you" (John 14:26). He speaks of the Trinity here.

THE HOLY SPIRIT AND CHRIST

Paul, when he was talking to believers in Rome, said; "You, however, are controlled not by the sinful nature but by the Spirit, if the Spirit of God lives in you. And *if* anyone does not have the Spirit of Christ, he does not belong to Christ" (Romans 8:9). His using the conjunction "if" should stir a question in our own minds about who controls our lives, if we say we have been saved. Is it the Holy Spirit or is it still our old sinful nature? This passage should also cause a stir in our hearts, and remind us that unless we have been born again by the Spirit of God, we continue to be controlled by our sinful nature.

When a person is baptized into Christ, he receives the gift of the Holy Spirit and now belongs to Christ. When a person is saved by the grace of God, through faith, the Holy Spirit comes into that person and gives him a new life. This new life then is ministered to, or counseled by, the Holy Spirit. Jesus said, "And I will ask the Father, and he will give you *another* Counselor to be with you forever—the Spirit of truth" (John 14:16,17). Did Jesus say another Counselor? He certainly did. Jesus, the Counselor, would ascend into heaven and the Father would then send the Holy Spirit, also called Counselor. This is further Scriptural evidence of another person, the person of the Holy Spirit.

Interestingly, as our own blood gives life to our physical body, it is Christ's shed blood that brings spiritual life to the person who believes in His death and resurrection. "... And without the shedding of blood there is no forgiveness" (Hebrews 9:22). God's forgiveness must come first, and then He gives us His Holy Spirit.

When does a person receive the Holy Spirit into his life? The gift of the Holy Spirit is given to anyone the moment they surrender their lives to Christ. (See chapter 8, Repentance, and Baptism).

RECEIVING THE HOLY SPIRIT

When Jesus reached the age of thirty, a time when His ministry was about to begin, He came to the river Jordan where John the Baptist was baptizing. To those who were there with John, John said, "I baptize you with water, but He [Jesus] will baptize you with the Holy Spirit" (Mark 1:8). This is exactly what happens today. When anyone in a church, in a public place, or in a private setting hears the call of God's saving grace being offered, and accepts the offer, Jesus sends the Holy Spirit into that person's life (Read Acts 2:38).

What does it mean to receive the gift of the Holy Spirit? It means that God in His miraculous way puts His Spirit into the new Christian. To receive the gift of the Holy Spirit means that the power of God is with the believer and the believer then is sealed by the Holy Spirit. "... with whom you were sealed for the day of redemption" (Ephesians 4:30).

THE SPIRIT GIVES LIFE

He brings new life into the newly converted person. Scriptures say, ".... but the Spirit gives birth to spirit" (John 3:6). This means the Holy Spirit is the one who gives the new Christian a new spiritual life. A person born of the Spirit has new life. Jesus said, "The Spirit gives life; the flesh counts for nothing. The words that I have spoken to you are spirit and they are life. Yet there are some of you who do not believe" (John 6:63,64). Note here the words of Jesus; "The flesh counts for nothing" means we cannot do one thing apart from the power of the Holy Spirit. *We cannot save ourselves or put ourselves right with God through religion, religious acts, good deeds, or works.*

GOD'S GRACE IS SHOWN THROUGH
THE HOLY SPIRIT

When one is saved by the grace of God, he will not fear physical death because he knows his soul and spirit will live forever. *God's grace, which is undeserved favor and above all, the power of God, enters the believer through the Holy Spirit.* It sounds almost too good to be true. Two things must precede such a glorious event as salvation, they are, repentance and faith. We are first born of the flesh which is our natural birth. When we are born of the Spirit, God spiritually adopts us. Romans 8:16 says, "The Spirit himself testifies with our spirit that we are God's children."

WHAT DOES IT MEAN TO BE BORN OF
WATER AND THE SPIRIT?

Jesus said to Nicodemus, "I tell you the truth, no one can enter the kingdom of God unless he is born of water and the Spirit" (John 3:5). There are three important things to think about.

32

(1)   Physical birth involves being born out of a pouch of water which is pure and clean.

(2)   Spiritual birth involves being born of the Spirit of God because " ... the Spirit gives life" (2 Corinthians 3:6).

(3)   Water baptism is necessary and is right with the Father. Jesus said, "...It is proper for us to do this..." (Matthew 3:15). He also said, "Flesh gives birth to flesh, but *the Spirit gives birth* to spirit," so we are born of the Holy Spirit (John 3:6).

The physical act of water baptism itself does not save a person. We are made pure and clean through God's forgiveness and grace. When the Holy Spirit enters into the person who has turned back (converted) to God, He will keep the believer pure as long as the believer lives in Him, and draws upon His presence and power. It is only through the Spirit's power that we are able to cut off any and all temptation.

When at the age of accountability, we accept, believe, and are baptized in water, we know that we are openly expressing our faith in Christ's death and resurrection. We also know, according to Scripture that "... He saved us through the washing of rebirth and renewal by the Holy Spirit, whom he poured out on us generously through Jesus Christ our Savior, so that, having been justified by his grace, we might become heirs having hope of eternal life" (Titus 3:5-6).

When we literally take the Holy Bible for what it is, which is God's truth, we know that without faith and obedience to God's Word, none of this means much.

GOD'S WORD ASSURES US THE FOLLOWING:

The Spirit of God saves us not by human effort, but by God's mercy through a washing (Titus 3:5-7).

The Holy Spirit is our witness that we are children of God (Romans 8:16).

Paul goes on to say that we are then justified by God's grace, and that we are made heirs according to the hope of eternal life (Titus 3:5-7).

33

THE HOLY SPIRIT'S EFFECT UPON THE BELIEVER

In essence, here is what happens when people are converted or born again. Their sins are forgiven and they no longer control their lives. How can this be? Romans 6:14 gives the answer: "For sin shall not be your master, because you are not under law, but under grace."

(1) *What law?* The law of sin and death (James 1:15).

(2) *What grace?* God's grace. Grace brings God's Power.

"In him we have redemption through his blood, the forgiveness of sins, in accordance with the riches of God's grace" (Ephesians 1:7).

It is only because of God's grace that we are given the Holy Spirit, and likewise, receive the kind of help we cannot give ourselves. Romans 6:18 tells us that the believer is made to be free from sin and is able to do things that are right with God.

Through the presence of the Holy Spirit, the followers of Christ are able to keep from sinning. How do they keep from sinning? We find the answer to this in 1 John 4:4. The apostle John is talking about those who are believers and followers of Christ. "You, dear children, are from God and have overcome them, because the one who is in you [Holy Spirit] is greater than the one [Satan] who is in the world." John's saying "you dear children" is referring to believers.

The Holy Spirit, who is God's power within the believer, makes the person sensitive to sin and keeps them from falling into sin. This is why it is important to know that "... in him we live and move and have our being" (Acts 17:28).

Though sin has no dominion over the believer, temptation is not ruled out. "...But if anybody does sin, we have the one who speaks to the Father in our defense—Jesus Christ, the Righteous One" (1 John 2:1). Drawing upon His presence, the Christian has great power in resisting temptation.

BELIEVERS ARE GIVEN A NEW LIFE

"And *if* the Spirit of him who raised Jesus from the dead is living in you, he who raised Christ from the dead will also give life to your mortal bodies through his Spirit, who lives in you" (Romans 8:11). The conjunction "if" appears again in Paul's writing. Examination of your personal position in Christ is worth looking into. Why? Because some profess Christ but have never confessed or acknowledged Him as their personal Savior. Some may consider themselves Christians but do not practice the presence of the Holy Spirit. It is only through *living in the Spirit* that we control our lives and allow God's grace to work. The believer's obligation is to live according to their faith in Christ, and then, through the Holy Spirit put to death the sinful misdeeds of the body.

HOW MANY GIFTS DOES THE BELIEVER RECEIVE?

The Bibles says that believers receive the gift of the Spirit. This gift then brings on other gifts. God's forgiveness is a gift. Other gifts are the promise of eternal life, the assurances of eternal life, the Grace period of the Church, the revelation of power of the word of the Holy Scriptures, and the Holy Spirit who teaches these truths to the believer. He is also the power source in our prayer life.

Drawing upon the Spirit's presence brings on the fruit of the Spirit, which is love, joy, peace, long suffering, gentleness, goodness, faith, meekness, and temperance. When these attributes are made alive in the believer, the presence of Christ begins to fill his life. Have you given Him his way in your life? Read Galatians 5:22-26.

GOD GIVES A WARNING ABOUT HOW WE TREAT THE HOLY SPIRIT

Jesus said in Matthew 12:32, "Anyone who speaks a word against the Son of Man will be forgiven, but anyone who speaks against the Holy Spirit will not be forgiven, either in this age or in the age to come." This grave and powerful announcement must not be shrugged off as unimportant.

The Holy Spirit is the express power of the Triune God. *It is critically important to know that we must never blaspheme against the Holy Spirit. Jesus said there is no forgiveness for this. To blaspheme means to deliberately speak or act irreverently against*

35

The Spirit of God. Contemptuous and irreverent acts are very dangerous and have consequences.

DEPARTING WORDS OF CHRIST REGARDING THE HOLY SPIRIT

Prior to leaving this earth and returning to the Father, Jesus gave us a most important promise concerning the Holy Spirit. He told the disciples that it would be appropriate for Him to go, because if He did not, He could not send us the Holy Spirit. Jesus said, "But I tell you the truth: It is for your good that I am going away. Unless I go away, the Counselor will not come to you; but if I go, I will send him to you. When he comes, he will convict the world of guilt in regard to sin and righteousness and judgment: in regard to sin, because men do not believe in me, in regard to righteousness, because I am going to the Father, where you can see me no longer" (John 16:7-10). Jesus, having said this, we know that prophecy was again fulfilled. It was Joel the prophet who said, "And afterward, I will pour my Spirit on all people" (Joel 2:28). [8th or 9th century BC].

CHRISTIANS GROW THROUGH THE HOLY SPIRIT

It is very important to know the means, which God provides, to help Christians grow spiritually. We learn the following from Jesus in John 16:13, "But when he, the Spirit of truth, comes, he will guide you into all truth ..." In Hebrews 6:1-6, Paul gave a discourse on the importance of spiritual progress. He said let's move forward from what we have come to know about our first Christian teachings of the doctrine of Jesus Christ. Let's not even think about laying a foundation of repentance, faith toward God, the doctrine of baptism, laying on of hands, the resurrection of the dead, and eternal judgment [paraphrasing mine]. Paul was not saying believers should ignore these important basics, but move ahead into a deeper knowledge of Christian maturity.

Living the faith means having a full dependency upon the Lord, through the indwelling of the Holy Spirit. Since we have God's love through Christ, the Christian is to live his life in the Spirit of Christ and in the love of God. In this way, the Christian will come to know Jesus in a more personal way. We must always remember that

Christian living means everything is centered in Christ.

DOES THE HOLY SPIRIT COME UPON BELIEVERS TODAY IN THE FORM OF A DOVE?

The Bible does not show any "descending dove" coming upon any convert. A dove came upon Jesus when he was baptized (John 1:32). The Bible does record other happenings and we will try to cover these events. First, let us turn to Acts 1:1-8 and Acts 2:1-4. After Jesus' resurrection, He showed Himself to the apostles and told them to wait in Jerusalem for the promise of the Father, who would send the Holy Spirit. The Holy Spirit then did come upon the disciples with tongues of fire. This was a fulfillment of what John the Baptist said, "... He will baptize you with the Holy Spirit and with fire" (Luke 3:16).

About one hundred and twenty disciples had received the Holy Spirit and were filled with His power. Believers today receive the gift of the Holy Spirit. Through Him, they have enough power and resources to lead a Christ-like life and then bear witness before others as to what Christ Jesus has done for them.

Jesus was crucified at the time of the Jewish Passover celebration or commemoration of the deliverance from Egypt, and He ascended forty days later. The Holy Spirit came fifty days after the crucifixion or ten days after the ascension.

Let us turn to Acts 2:31-42. Peter's sermon to the Jews was straightforward and with power from the Holy Spirit. He told them that they had crucified Jesus, whom God sent. This pricked their hearts, and then they asked Peter what they should do. Peter told them to repent and be baptized in the name of Jesus Christ for the remission of sins, and *they would receive the gift of the Holy Spirit.* Three thousand souls were converted that day. Then they continued steadfastly in the apostles' doctrine and fellowship, in breaking bread, and in prayers. Luke, the writer of Acts, does not mention any baptism by water in this account. He does, though, bring in water baptism in this next account.

In Acts 10:34-48 we see a progression of events as Peter preached the gospel of Jesus Christ, and said whoever believes will receive forgiveness for their sins. "While Peter was still speaking these words the Holy Spirit came on all who heard the message" (vs 44). Those Jews and Gentiles, who believed, received the Holy Spirit. Importantly, after the new believers expressed belief in the Word preached by Peter, they received the gift of the Holy Spirit. Then they spoke in tongues. Peter then said (vs 47), "Can anyone keep these people from being baptized with water?" *The order of these events reveal water baptism as having taken place after they had received the Holy Spirit.*

God's grace is shown through the Holy Spirit. He is the power that raised Christ from the dead and is the same Spirit who comes into believers today. He is equal with Father and Son. He is the Spirit of Christ, of Glory, Grace, Promise and Wisdom. Whether we speak of Him as Revealer, Intercessor, Reprover, or Comforter, He, the Holy Spirit, is all in all.

THE HOLY SPIRIT HAS SEALED THE BELIEVER'S SALVATION

"And do not grieve the Holy Spirit of God, with whom you were sealed for the day of redemption" (Ephesians 4:30). "Sealed" indicates a locking in, or a preservation. Believers are very fortunate to have the "anointing" of the Holy Spirit and to know their salvation is indisputable.

The Holy Spirit bears witness to Christ's coming by water and blood. "... And it is the Spirit who testifies, because the Spirit is the truth" (1 John 5:6). The Holy Spirit came upon Jesus when He began His ministry. He comes into new Christians at the precise moment of their conversion. (Read Acts 2:38, 10:44).

OLD TESTAMENT TELLS OF A NEW LIFE THROUGH THE SPIRIT

When Jesus said to Nicodemus, "You must be born again," we do not know if Nicodemus associated God's promise written in the book of Ezekiel with this new life. Although he was a teacher of the Old Testament, we do not know what his thoughts were. The book of Ezekiel (36:24-28) tells of how God would give Israel a new life. He promised them a better place to live through a cleansing with water, giving them a new heart and putting His Spirit within them to help live within the statutes of the Lord and thusly help them to live apart from sin. God would always be Israel's God and better things are yet to come. God puts His Spirit into all believers to help them live apart from sin, through the sensitivity of his Holy presence.

The Holy Spirit is seen actively in the Old Testament with Samson: "The Spirit of the Lord came upon him in power..." (Judges 14:6). The Holy Spirit came upon many in Old Testament times to empower them. How fortunate are the true believers of today.

THE HOLY SPIRIT MOVED:

Upon men of old time to write the Bible,

Upon all of God's servants,

Upon Jesus' ministry,

Upon the disciples,

Upon believers of all time,

Upon all men who kept His statutes,

Upon the Virgin Mary,

Upon all truth seekers,

Upon Christ toward heaven, and

Upon new believers.

The Holy Spirit does not come into people because they are good. He comes into them because they have confessed Jesus Christ as their Savior. *Salvation does not come by association, gathering, or church traditions. It comes through individual commitment and above all, the grace of God.* Have you searched your heart? Have you committed yourself to Jesus Christ?

GOD'S ABUNDANT KINDNESS
Ephesians 1:1-14 records three important events:

God's Plan of Salvation. Verses 4 and 5 tell us of God's love in choosing to save man for His own good pleasure.

Revelation of the Divine Mystery. Verse 10 tells us that God through Christ would bring us to Himself.

39

The **Believer's Spiritual Heritage.** Verses 11 and 13 assure believers that through Christ they receive an inheritance. And because they heard and believed the word of truth about Jesus Christ, they are sealed, or preserved, by the Holy Spirit Himself. Believers then live in peace because God gives freedom to those who are His. The Holy Spirit must never be watered down or minimized, set aside or forgotten. Christians must never grieve the Holy Spirit.

A FRIEND RECEIVES THE HOLY SPIRIT

I once met a man who thought he was born again, but was not quiet sure. He knew very little about why he might be saved. He said that he just followed the crowd when a salvation call was made in an outdoor arena. When I told him what it said in Romans 10:9 and 10, about confessing and believing in Christ's resurrection, and that this is how we are saved, he quickly made his confession to salvation. He now believes he is saved beyond a question of a doubt. Acts 10:44 came to my mind. "While Peter was still speaking these words, the Holy Spirit came on all who heard the message." I knew my friend heard the Word of God as I used it in my witness to him.

Many become saved and receive the Holy Spirit when they truly listen and hear what the Word of God is saying. How about you? When you read the Word of God, are you listening or just reading?

OUR BELIEF TODAY

God's promises have not changed. He offers a cleansing and restoration to all people. Personal belief in Christ will usher in the power of the Holy Spirit to all who will confess Him as Savior. "... Believe in the Lord Jesus and you will be saved." (Read John 16:29-31).

Spiritual immersion into Christ through faith assures us of God's promise, that He will be our God forever. We are born into a new spirit by the Holy Spirit who gives us Himself when we ask with true belief.

..."If you then, though you are evil, know how to give good gifts to your children, how much more will your Father in Heaven give the Holy Spirit to those who ask him!" (Luke 11:13)

CHAPTER 5

SIN

Physical death is certain. Sin brings with it a spiritual death. This death is a separation from God. It is a terrible thing to be separated from God. Unless sin is dealt with while there is still time, there is no hope. Conversely, there is hope for the sinner, and this hope rests in a personal redemption, which means to be bought back to God. Christ's death on the cross has made possible redemption or a buy back. Why? Because "... Sin entered the world through one man, and death through sin, and in this way death came to all men, because all have sinned" (Romans 5:12). Why Christ? Because "Salvation is found in no one else, for there is no other name under heaven given to men by which we must be saved" (Acts 4:12). What did Christ's death do? Paul said that believers were bought at a price (1 Corinthians 6:20). Jesus paid the price for the sins of everyone, for all time. (Read John 3:16)

This will not be a very popular chapter. I often think about the reason why some people dislike hearing the Word of God. Some people do not like to have sinful things pointed out to them because there are far too many pleasurable things that bring them satisfaction. Sexual pleasures outside of marriage, wanting what others have, greed, and most anything which satisfies our wants, continue to motivate the sinful nature of people. In wanting to satisfy our five senses—touch, taste, smell, hearing, and seeing—people are forever preoccupied with personal pleasures. The kind of pleasures that lead to sin will always separate us from God. To do wrong to family, friends, and neighbors, by nature of these sins, will never satisfy the tie that binds people together. Instead, the flame of love diminishes and we sink deeper and deeper into insensibility that leads us to calloused and ungodly behavior. Perhaps most of us, if we were truthful, would have to admit we've been down this trail before. The Christian man, woman, boy, or girl should by every means find that victory over sin.

SIN AND TEMPTATION

Sin detaches us from those we love and, above all, from God. Sin started with Eve and Adam when they disobeyed God and ate of the fruit of the forbidden tree. The Lord God commanded the man not to eat from the tree of knowledge of good and evil (Genesis 2:16-17). Satan tempted Eve, then Adam and Eve fell, and sin was conceived. Temptation is not sin. Our best defense in any temptation that leads to sin is obedience to the Word of God. Jesus was tempted, but did not succumb to Satan's temptation.

When believers pray often and live in harmony with Christ's teachings they become very sensitive to all things which are sin. Those who live for Christ please God and fulfill His righteousness. Obedience to Christ's call to repentance and belief in Him, bring changes in behavior and attitude. Calmness, and a new kind of freedom is realized such as you never had before. Obedience means we submit to controlling our will toward those things that are right with the principles of right or wrong.

THE ROAD TO VICTORY

If through our wants and desires we make ourselves captive to wrongdoing, then why not just say no to wrongdoing? Anything which is not right with God is wrongdoing and is sin (1 John 5:17). When we decide to say no to sin, we can be sure God will be there to help us. There is only one sure way we can free ourselves from sin—call upon the name of Christ Jesus and He will free you.

Romans 5:12-21 discloses the reign of sin, how it separates us from God, and brings with it condemnation. Man has a sinful nature, and it is only through a spiritual change from within that the Holy Spirit is able to help the believer at a time of temptation.

Jesus' personal invitation through the Word tells us how that can be changed. He said, "I tell you the truth, no one can see the kingdom of God unless he is born again" (John 3:3). To be born again is to acquire a spiritual change by the grace of God. Paul told the Roman Christians (Romans 6:6-9) that their sins were crucified with Jesus and the power of sin no longer had a hold over them.

THE "SELF" DEFENSE
There are people who feel it is not right for God to judge them

because of Adam's sin, yet every one of us prove to be equal with Adam by our sins. Man, though having inherited his tendency to sin through Adam, has also, through Jesus Christ's atoning death and resurrection, been given a means for restoration with God. This cannot be over emphasized, because it is God's will that all people be saved from hell (1 Timothy 2:4). It is only through believing upon Christ's birth, death, and resurrection that man is given power through the Holy Spirit, to keep himself from sin. "For sin shall not be your master, because you are not under law (meaning not under the power of sin), but under grace" (Romans 6:14). Spiritual liberty is given to those who believe in the only man who could ever transform lives, and that man is Jesus Christ. As He is "The Truth," He will make you free. Obedience to His Word is vital (John 8:31,32).

TRUE FREEDOM AND BEING A SLAVE TO SIN

Spiritual liberty is man having been made free to enjoy a life fully dedicated to God, and living with the hope of eternal life (Romans 6:12). It was during a period in Israel's history known as the time of the Judges, that we learn about sin and its consequences. In those days, everyone did what they thought was right or wrong. Opinions and self-rule of authority brought about frightening results.

It is when we make decisions apart from the Word of God, which contain the rules for right living, that we end up in sin, which brings moral decay. When sin runs rampant, many people suffer the aftermath. Because of man's conscience, sin is unpopular. Many people have attested to the emptiness in their lives, and don't know what to do about it. Our sins always condemn us. We usually know when we do wrong. It is only when we become emotionally hardened through continual sinning that we enter into a denial state of right versus wrong. The believer is given power from the Holy Spirit to overcome temptation which leads to sin (1 John 3:9). Sin is universal, and if we say that we have no sin because we may think we're good, we deceive ourselves, and the truth is not in us (1 John 5:19).

SIN DEFINED

Sin, according to the Word of God, is defined: "All wrongdoing is sin..." (1 John 5:17). We know that anything which is not right with

God is sin. Sin may be defined as transgression, or a breach of God's laws (1 John 3:4). Omission, or oversight of right or wrong, does not excuse us. We look at "wrong" as sin, yet sin can be not doing what we may know to be right. An example of this is when we have a close friend who may need help, and we decide to look the other way. When we know something is wrong and still do it, it is called a sin of commission. When we know it is right to do something and then not do it, it is called a sin of omission (James 4:17). "...everything that does not come from faith is sin" (Romans 14:23). We must be careful not to look down on other Christians when they do not follow the Scriptures as we think they ought to.

POWER FROM ABOVE

Sources of sin are found in the following: Submission to Satan's many traps, the lust of the flesh, obsession with physical desires and materialism, lust of the eyes, or the pride of life (1 John 2:16). A believer who has been baptized in the Holy Spirit has a special kind of power over sin. This power is from God Himself. (Baptized here means to be immersed spiritually into Christ.)

Believing means to trust, follow, and obey. Those who obey find power over sin through their faith in the Spirit's presence. Sin does not have dominion over the true followers of Christ because they are under grace (Romans 6:14). The Apostle John says, "No one who is born of God will continue to sin, because God's seed remains in him; he cannot go on sinning, because he has been born of God" (1 John 3:9).

A LOOK AT WHAT THE
SCRIPTURES SAY ABOUT SINS

"Righteousness exalts a nation, but sin is a disgrace to any people" (Proverbs 14:34). Any nation influenced by God's commandments is blessed.

PERSONAL SINS: "But if anybody does sin, we have one who speaks to the Father in our defense—Jesus Christ..." (1 John 2:1). It is evident that John wrote this for the believer's ears. His opening words are "My dear children," meaning children of God.

SINS DONE IN SECRET: Jesus said, "But I tell you that anyone who looks at a woman lustfully has already committed adultery with her in his heart" (Matthew 5:28). Eye sinning is common today.

SELF—DECEPTION: "If we claim to be without sin, we deceive ourselves and the truth is not in us" (1 John 1:8). If we were to write out a truthful list of our sins, we may discover our insensitivity to sin.

SIN— IS IT WORTH IT?

The effects of sinning can be a terrible thing in a person's life. If you are plagued by specific kinds of sins, now would be the time to do something about it. Coming to realize the great penalty before it's too late is smart. What are some of these sins? Immoral acts, wickedness, allowing any specific thing or object to be more meaningful than our personal communion with God, sex outside of marriage, lovers of same sex, stealing, greediness, drunkenness, lying, slandering, or anything which is not right with God. You know the old saying, "What's it going to cost me?" In this case, it could be your life. The Bible records what God has to say about sin: the kingdom of heaven is out of reach. Only Christ can put away our sins.

SIN'S COST AND MAN'S RECOURSE

God presents us with this question: "Do you not know that the wicked will not inherit the kingdom of God?" (1 Corinthians 6:9). The unrighteous are the unsaved, that is, those whose sins were not yet made right before God. The cost will be unbearable. Why? Because it brings death and hell and torment. You may ask, "What can I do about it?" Get yourself reconciled or made right, with God. He loves us in spite of our sins, and has provided a means to clear our slate.

Coming to know God's love for us and His grace through Jesus Christ is a first big step. We must surrender ourselves to Christ because only He can put away our sins. We must not be confused with man's simplistic formulas to salvation. God does not save us so that we can become financially wealthy and gain in material possessions, as some have preached. No, He wants us to be made right with Him, so that He will not have to send us to hell. We become God's children first; then we learn how to live a right kind of life and how to love God. **God takes us as we are, then as his children he helps us to change.**

45

Listen to what Paul had to say about these things as he addressed the believers at Galatia: "For all of you who were baptized into Christ have clothed yourselves with Christ" (Galatians 3:27). What does this mean? To be baptized into Christ and to clothe ourselves with Christ is more than an emotional ascent to godliness. So then, how do we do this? First, by surrendering ourselves to Christ, secondly, by living according to His laws. When our sins are forgiven, we are able to serve our Lord.

It was after Paul had received his call from the Lord that he was pressed into service to God. Ananias, the man whom God had chosen to talk to Paul after Paul gave his life to Christ, said; "And now what are you waiting for? Get up, be baptized and wash your sins away, calling on his name" (Acts 22:16).

NEW LEASE ON LIFE (The Good News)

The person regenerated by the grace of God has been forgiven and restored. Because of his new nature (power over sin), and having been baptized (meaning immersed into Jesus Christ both in his death, and in his resurrection) he is able to be in Christ spiritually. By the same power that raised Jesus from the dead, the power of the Holy Spirit, we also maintain our newly restored position in the body of Christ.

Because this was done by God the Father, we can walk in the knowledge of the newness of life. "Born again" means a new spiritual life has been given through faith and, above all through God's grace (Romans 6:3,4).

"Therefore, if anyone is in Christ, he is a new creation; the old has gone, the new has come!" (2 Corinthians 5:17).

GOD'S MIRACLE AND HIS GRACE

What becomes new? Your life becomes new. Why? Because you are in Christ. When you set before Him the sins of your life and say, "I will turn away from sin" and mean it, you have a new kind of life. When you believe in your heart that Jesus was raised from the dead after He was crucified, you can know that you have just become a new creature in Christ. Your sins have been washed away by the blood of

Christist. ***God's miracle and grace have come over you.*** Through your sincere personal confession, and promise to turn away from your old sinful life you are brought back to God. What is meant by, "brought back"? The Bible tells us that we are His to start with. It is sin that separates us from Him. This next passage is an important reminder to believers who hate to sin. "Because through Christ Jesus the law of the Spirit of life set me free from the law of sin and death" (Romans 8:2). The believer having been given the gift of the Holy Spirit has God's power to live a righteous life. This new life rests entirely upon the only means God has provided, his Son Jesus Christ.

FREE FROM THE POWER OF SIN AND DEATH

What does God mean when He says he will not condemn or judge us when we are in Christ? The passage, "Therefore, there is now no condemnation for those who are in Christ Jesus, because through Christ Jesus the Law of the Spirit of life set me free from the law of sin and death" (Romans 8:1,2). The Word of God does not lie. The Holy Spirit sets us free. "... But the Spirit gives life" (2 Corinthians 3:6). The law of sin and death is easily explained. Your sins will kill you unless you allow them to be justified through believing in Christ the Savior. Yes, God has made it that easy, just believe upon Christ Jesus.

AFTERMATH OF SIN AND AFTERMATH OF SALVATION

We cannot address sin without understanding its consequences. Sin comes from satisfying fleshly appetites and fulfilling selfish needs, or filling the desires of an evil spirit. The aftermath of sin is hell. The aftermath of God's grace is a new life. Those who are immersed in Christ are preserved in Christ. They pass from a no-win plight to a new and secure life.

JESUS, IN EFFECT, SAYS, "YOU HAVE MY WORD ON IT"

Jesus said in John 5:24, "I tell you the truth, whoever hears my word and believes him who sent me has eternal life and will not be condemned; he has crossed over from death to life." Two important points to think about here. ***First,*** the "crossed over from death" means that man is no longer separated from God because he has been restored. ***Secondly,*** the "to life" refers to eternal life. Here again we see God's promise of full restoration to those who have been redeemed by the blood of Christ.

THE BIBLE SAYS, SHALL WE CONTINUE TO SIN?

"What shall we say, then? Shall we go on sinning so that grace may increase? By no means! We died to sin; how can we live in it any longer?" (Romans 6:1,2).

Let us examine the Scriptures concerning this delicate and hard to understand subject of sinning after you have been saved by the Grace of God.

(1) *"Born of God."* The Bible says in 1 John 3:9, "No one who is born of God will continue to sin, because God's seed remains in him; he cannot go on sinning, because he has been born of God."

(2) *"Have crucified the sinful nature."* "Those who belong to Christ Jesus have crucified the sinful nature with its passions and desires. Since we live by the Spirit, let us keep in step with the Spirit" (Galatians 5:24,25). God's word says it all here. However, there are two important views to consider. *One*, just what do you and I plan to do with our new walk in Christ? Here is where we must quit kidding ourselves. Are we walking in step with the Spirit's presence? *Two*, if, we play religion, then we are no better than the Pharisees whom Jesus chastised. On the outside, they pretended to be good; on the inside, they were rotten. We cannot play on both sides of the fence anymore than they did.

In regard to our "obedience" to what Christ did for us at the cross. True Christians work their faith through their own initiative and determination. They live by faith and trust and know that the Holy Spirit is "the source" of their power. *When the Christian works his faith, he will continually experience victory over sin through his faith.* If he should fall into sin again, the believer and follower, who is under God's grace, will come to Jesus and confess his specific sins. Jesus will speak to God the Father in his defense. Jesus takes care of His own. The Bible says, "But if anybody does sin, we have one who speaks to the Father in our defense—Jesus Christ the Righteous One..." (1 John 2:1). Christ's servant Peter saluted those Christians that had received their faith, which Peter said was the same as his (2 Peter 1:1). We must encourage other Christians to believe what God has given them, such as, faith and grace, and the Holy Spirit to help them to keep their fellowship with God open at all times. God's divine power gives believers everything they need —for life.

THE BELIEVER'S RELATIONSHIP AND FELLOWSHIP WITH GOD

Through obedience, we are able to maintain our fellowship with God. Our relationship with God is kept safe because of His gift to us, which is the gift of the Holy Spirit or God's power within us. When we override His presence or commit sin, we must immediately come to Christ and ask His intercession before the Father.

God's seed, the Holy Spirit, remains in the believer. When God gave us the gift of the Holy Spirit at the moment of our conversion, he did not take away our freedom of choice. Our relationship stands firm, but sin breaks our fellowship with God.

CHRIST'S TEACHING ON HOW WE FIGHT SIN

"And lead us not into temptation, but deliver us from the evil one" (Matthew 6:13). Let us remember that Jesus taught this prayer to the disciples, and it applies to believers today. When we pray this part of Jesus' teaching, on how we can have victory over sin, we must not recite this verse of Scripture with meaningless chatter, but with the full confidence that God will deliver us out of any temptation that will lead to sin. Also, He gave us His Spirit to help us; we have no excuses. The apostle John wrote, "If we confess our sins, he is faithful and just and will forgive us our sins and purify us from all unrighteousness" (1 John 1:9).

JESUS OVERCAME

Temptation may be right in front of you as it was with Jesus, but as long as you draw upon the Spirit within you, you will not sin. Jesus said, "... just as I overcame ..." (Revelation 3:21). Jesus was tempted of the devil after He was filled with the Holy Spirit and so are all believers. Satan does not have to work too hard on the unbelieving. He works doubly hard upon the faithful followers of Christ. Be prepared to know we can do everything through Christ. He gives us the strength (Philippians 4:13).

PAUL'S FAITH IS EXPRESSED TO ALL BELIEVERS

Listen to the encouraging words from the apostle Paul, who also was filled with the Holy Spirit, "The Lord will rescue me from every evil attack and will bring me safely to His heavenly kingdom. To Him be glory forever and ever. Amen." (2 Timothy 4:18). Evilness is not only found in the remote areas of the world where voodoo is practiced, but also in the hearts of men everywhere, and in many different forms. Evil is anything that works against the righteousness of God. Sin is evil. Evil is any force that opposes God and His work of righteousness in the world. Believers are running a race and they want to win the prize (meaning to receive the gift of life). God has given the believer His Holy Spirit to come to know the truth of the written Word of God.

God has given the believer everything and still has not taken away his freedom of choice. The real and true freedom though is in Christ.

RUNNING A GOOD RACE

Paul gives an excellent illustration concerning running a race, and comparing physical readiness with spiritual readiness. Many great sport stars through out time may have had their trophies to polish and cherish, but they cannot take these with them. They put their bodies through a lot of punishment only to find that in the end, the glory only lasted a very short time. Paul tells us in 1 Corinthians 9:25-27, "Everyone who competes in the games goes into strict training. They do it to get a crown that will not last; but we do it to get a crown that will last forever. Therefore, I do not run like a man running aimlessly; I do not fight like a man beating the air. No, I beat my body and make it my slave so that after I have preached to others, I myself will not be disqualified for the prize."

THE BELIEVERS ADVANTAGE

As believers, we are running the race of our lives and we have been given a superior position. This advantage is in the power of the indwelling Holy Spirit. When we let Him direct our lives through prayer and acknowledging His presence, we are taken out of many difficult situations. Paul told the Galatians, "... Live by the Spirit and you will not gratify the desires of the sinful nature" (Galatians 5:16). Life is a matter of flesh against Spirit and Spirit against flesh (Verse 17). Faith, though, is the heartbeat of our religion.

Paul reminded the Corinthians of what happened to the Jews after their exodus from Egypt. God freed them from four hundred years of slavery to the Pharaoh of Egypt. They were enroute to the land of milk and honey and still they forgot God's grace and mercy. They soon began to live in sin which displeased God. He told them to be aware of temptations common to man. God fortifies the believer and limits Satan through divine protection which provides an escape from situations which otherwise would make them fall. God is faithful to those who follow Him and will not let them be tempted above that which they can handle. "... And God is faithful; he will not let you be tempted beyond what you can bear..." (1 Corinthians 10:13). He will make a way for you to escape. Anyone who is without the Holy Spirit is on his own, and that is why it is so vitally important to become a faithful and true believer, and follower of Jesus Christ. Believers today have a distinct advantage in the battle of sinful temptations.

THE BIBLE SAYS, DO NOT QUENCH THE SPIRIT

Paul, who is talking to the believers in Thessalonica, addresses the sin of quenching the Spirit. He reminds them of the day of the Lord. It's obvious he's talking to believers. He said in 1 Thessalonians 5:4, "But you, **brothers**, are not in darkness so that this day should surprise you like a thief. You are all the **sons of light** [believers] and sons of the day." He told them in verse 8 to be self-controlled. Obviously, this meant they had to apply something from within themselves— obedience. In verse 9, he told them, "For God did not appoint us to suffer wrath but to receive salvation through our Lord Jesus Christ."

Then in verses 14 through 22 he exhorted them to live according to their Christian duties. He encouraged them to pray without ceasing, and to give God thanks for everything, because it is God's will to do so. Next, he said, "Do not put out the Spirit's fire." In other words, don't put the Spirit out: don't extinguish Him. God does not give His Holy Spirit to anyone, only to believers. The Spirit is given to the elect of God. If you are a believer, then you are the elect. Remember, salvation is for all who will believe, and belief involves hearing, and doing what the Word of God says, through obedience.

PUTTING ON THE WHOLE ARMOR OF GOD

The apostle Paul, writing to believers at Ephesus, said, "Finally, be strong in the Lord and his mighty power. Put on the full armor of God, so that you can take your stand against the devil's schemes" (Ephesians 6:10,11). To be strong in the Lord means to draw upon the Holy Spirit's power that is within you through your faith. He said we are to put on the whole armor of God. The whole armor is represented in everything God has given the newly converted person.

THE ARMOR

1. Live life in truth.
2. Live in peace.
3. Live in faith.
4. Live by the Word of God through obedience to it.
5. Live ready to tell others about Christ.

SCRIPTURES KEPT IN CONTEXT

"For all have sinned and fall short of the Glory of God" (Romans 3:23). Who is the "all" referred to here? All who have become of an accountable age before they are saved. It is this writer's belief that God will not condemn a child who has not reached the age of accountability. However, when a child does reach the age of accountability, he or she has reached the age of responsibility. Man is liable for his sins, and the consequence, which follow. This aftermath results in judgment and death. This death means torment and separation from God after the day of final judgment. Man is in a depraved condition or morally corrupt, from the start. Unless a conversion by the power of the Cross takes place, the lake of burning fire and sulfur await man (Revelation 21:8). To the victor, God promises He will be their God, and they will be His son.

THE SEVEN CONDITIONS OF MAN
(From separation to restoration)

(1) Man's sins separate him from God.
(2) Man's helplessness is due to his sinful state.
(3) Man's Savior is the result of God's grace.
(4) Man's repentance is his turning away from sin.
(5) Man's confession is his surrender to Christ.
(6) Man's restoration means he's been returned to God.
(7) Man's inheritance is the gift of life.

TAKING A PERSONAL INVENTORY

Where do you stand? Is your name in the Book of Life? There is one way to be certain. Surrender your life to Christ. Make up your mind that from this point forward anything, which is sin, is your enemy. Come to believe that Christ's resurrection gives us the hope of living with God forever. Don't put it off any longer. Make your claim for the inheritance of your lifetime. It requires only a tiny amount of faith to call upon the name of Jesus Christ. Our great enemy is pride. Self–importance, arrogance, or an attitude of self–sufficiency create a wide space between man and God. God is then saddened even further because He wants all people to come to Him. God is waiting for the unsaved, as He wants everyone to be restored through His only Son, Jesus Christ. We always have a choice.

MAKING A PERSONAL COMMITMENT AND DECISION

Simply say, "Yes, Jesus, I want you to come into my life. I am a sinner, and I want and need your forgiveness. My desire, with your help, is to change my life by doing your will. I do believe my sins died with you on the cross. I believe you were resurrected from the grave so that I might live forever. I believe in the written Word, and call upon your name. I want your written Word to become the living Word in Me. I do believe you are the Christ who died for me because you love me." Upon saying this prayer in truth, before God, you've made your decision and by God's Grace, dear friend, you've been saved by Grace.

TRUSTWORTHY INSTRUCTIONS WORTH RECALLING

If you are a believer, then perhaps you will remember what Paul said to the believers at Rome: "Now if we died with Christ, we believe that we will also live with him. For we know that since Christ was raised from the dead, he cannot die again; death no longer has mastery over him. The death he died, he died to sin once and for all; but the life he lives, he lives to God. In the same way count yourselves dead to sin but alive to God in Christ Jesus. Therefore, do not let sin reign in your mortal body so that you obey its evil desires. Do not offer the parts of your body to sin, as instruments of wickedness, but rather offer yourselves to God, as those who have been brought from death to life; and offer the parts of your body to him as instruments of righteousness. For sin shall not be your master, because you are not under law, but under grace" (Romans 6:8-14).

Obviously, this passage was written to believers, to assure them, that once the line is crossed to come to Christ, you are in God's hands. How about you, have you crossed the line to come to Christ? The choice is yours.

If you choose to cross the line to come to Christ right at this very moment, you will be making the best decision of your life. No, you will not have to become an expert in the Bible, or suddenly become "holier than thou" so to speak. Why not turn back one page and read about the personal commitment that you must make in order to be freed from the power of the devil. Make up your mind now and God will do the rest. He will give you all spiritual blessings. Take the time right now and read the first chapter of the book of Ephesians. Here you will find the riches of your inheritance. When you do accept Christ know this— you belong to Him and him alone, because we find our restoration to God through Christ Jesus. That is, through our faith and his grace and not by anything we do, such as works and good deeds. We are saved by grace through faith: Nothing we do of ourselves, except submission to our wonderful and loving God, can bring us to Him.

"That if you confess with your mouth, Jesus Christ is Lord, and believe in your heart that God raised him from the dead, you will be saved" (Romans 10-9).

CHAPTER 6

FAITH

Jesus tells us to have faith and not doubt. He says that if we believe in what we believe, it will happen. He says, "Have faith in God" (Mark 11:22-23). Paul tells the Galatians, "But the Scripture declares that the whole world is a prisoner of sin, so that what was promised, *being given through faith* in Jesus Christ, *might be given* to those who believe" (Galatians 3:22). From this passage, we learn that God gives faith to us, and He gives it to anyone the moment they believe.

Faith is the stimulus of Christianity. It is a moving power expressed from within the believer. Faith brings with it the power to have victory over sin and the power to overcome or defeat the world. The one who believes in Jesus Christ overcomes the world (1 John 5:5).

Faith, to be faith, must be functional. It is through faith and grace that we are saved. Belief without proof is the faith that binds all believers in the doctrine of Jesus Christ.

WHAT REALLY IS FAITH?

The Bible tells us this about faith: "Now faith is being sure of what we hope for and certain of what we do not see" (Hebrews 11:1). Study of the Bible discloses faith as the most needed thing to please God (Hebrews 11:6), and to find spiritual restoration. *Without faith*, salvation is hopeless. *Without faith*, man's religion is empty. *Without faith*, truth of God's word is ineffective. *Without faith*, we would have no walk with God. Is there a difference between faith and feelings? The contrast should be understood and applied accordingly. Feelings deal with emotions and physical sensations. Faith deals with internal assurances of things which we hope for.

WHERE IS FAITH FOUND?

In our quest to know its spiritual significance, we know that faith is found only through the Holy Spirit. It does not rest upon men's wisdom (1 Corinthians 2:15; 12:9). When the Spirit of God sees the desire of the heart and intent toward Christ the seed of faith is given. Where it is true that all believers have faith, some are given a deeper

55

faith. Why? "To prepare God's people for works of service, so that the body of Christ may be built up until we all reach unity in the faith and in the knowledge of the Son of God and become mature, attaining to the whole measure of the fullness of Christ" (Ephesians 4:12,13). We first become believers and then through our love, serve God. Other gifts, including a deeper faith, may be given.

Faith is not found in the church, although it is possible that through the church one will find faith. The Christian's faith is grounded in the person of Jesus Christ. Those who have been baptized spiritually into Christ are in a very different position than those who have not been spiritually reborn. Why? God looks at the believers and followers of Jesus as if they died with Christ. God calls His own, "saints". Faith is expressed when the Gospel of Christ is shared with others. Galatians 2:20 clearly defines this. Christ lives in our hearts by our faith. A saving faith is not found in the pastor, the saints, priests, evangelists, deacons, preachers or teachers. Faith is found only in the person of Jesus Christ, in what He did at the cross and what He will do when He comes for His body of Believers. Faith binds Christians together. Through their collective faith, the Church is living in a period of God's grace.

PREVAILING FAITH

There is good reason to have faith in Jesus Christ and in Him alone. Think, if you will, about what Jesus said in John 14:6, "I am the way and the truth, and the life. No man comes to the Father except through me." What specifically did He mean by this? Jesus is not about the truth; *He is the truth.* We may talk about the truth of anything, we may be truthful; but Jesus is the truth. *He is the only way to God the Father, and He is life itself.* By saying He is the life, Jesus is telling everyone that He is life itself. Anyone wanting to have life eternal can have it through Him by faith. *"Through him all things were made; without him nothing was made that has been made" (John 1:3).* Jesus is the Alpha and the Omega, the beginning and the end, as recorded in Revelation 22:13. Millions of people who do not practice Christianity are blind to these truths. It is obvious they do not have the same faith in the Word of God that Christians do.

FINDING FAITH

How does one get faith? The Word of God tells us how we can receive the most important spiritual element needed to change our lives, which is faith. It says, "Consequently, faith comes from hearing the message, and *the message is heard through the word of Christ* (Romans 10:17). To listen means to make a conscious effort to want to hear the message of Christ. Man is free to accept or reject the message. However, if, you want to have faith and you make a conscious effort to hear what God's Word says, *then you will hear the Word of Christ and get faith.* Many people seemingly listen, but do not hear what the Word is saying. Obviously, they don't want to hear the message. An example is when our children hear us but do not do what we say.

His Words of the Bible are as alive today just as they were when first inspirationally written. Jesus said, "Heaven and earth will pass away, but my words will never pass away" (Mark 13:31). The words of the Holy Bible are the very words of Jesus, and they are the words that shall never pass away. *With many, there is a lack of faith in God's words of the Bible.* "... faith comes from hearing the message, and the message is heard through the word of Christ" Romans 10:17). Faith is a product of belief, and when we know for certain that we believe, we know that our conviction and confidence has been established. When faith in the Word of God is working, the Holy Spirit makes known its truths. "... But when he, the Spirit of truth, comes, he will guide you into all truth" (John 16:13). Satan knows this and is out to destroy our faith in the laws of God.

FAITH—AS A MEASURE OF MAN'S BELIEF

Faith is expressed in a belief which comes from within the spirit of the person toward the Word of God. Men with faith in God's laws will reflect this in the common laws of the land. The Constitution of the United States is based upon God's laws. Many of man's laws have been put ahead of God's laws. God will not tolerate these changes any more today, than He did in the days of Sodom and Gomorrah. *Faith comes from the Word of God, and what man does with his faith is a measure of his belief.* Anyone with faith in the Word of God will find

57

the will of God in their life. God's standards become their guidelines.

Without faith, it is impossible to please God. Jesus places believing as most necessary to find favor with God. Jesus told the young girl which He had healed after she merely touched His clothes, "... Don't be afraid; just believe" (Mark 5:36). Believing in Jesus Christ means to trust, follow and obey Him in all aspects of life. Without the Bible, man has no means to the truth. How so? Jesus plainly says, "I am the way and the truth..." (John 14:6).

FAITH AND MIRACLES
JESUS RAISES LAZARUS FROM THE DEAD

Jesus raised a dead man from the grave four days after he died. As with all of Jesus' miracles, there was a purpose for this one. It was to confirm to the disciples who Jesus said He was—the Messiah. Jesus told the disciples, "... Our friend Lazarus has fallen asleep; but I am going there to wake him up. His disciples replied, Lord, if he sleeps, he will get better. Jesus had been speaking of Lazarus's death, but his disciples' thought he meant natural sleep. So then, he told them plainly, Lazarus is dead, and for your sake, I am glad I was not there, so that you may believe. But let us go to him" (John 11:11-15).

If Lazarus were just sick, healing him would not have been as significant a testimony as bringing back a dead body, which was decomposed four days (verse 17). No man could have this kind of power except the divine Christ.

Martha's faith in Jesus proves to be very strong. She says to Jesus, "If you had been here, my brother would not have died" (John 11:21). Martha knew the truth and believed Jesus without proof, which is a true faith. If man were not so stubborn and full of self-pride, he would need no proof for everything which the Bible claims. Jesus often said to those about Him "believe in me." The Jews in the Temple asked Jesus, "How long will you keep us in suspense? If you are the Christ, tell us plainly. Jesus answered, I did tell you, but you do not believe. The miracles I do in my Father's name speak for me..." (John 10:24-25).

It was when Jesus had performed His first miracle, turning water

58

into wine, that the disciples believed in Jesus. This is confirmed in John 2:11; it reads: "This, the first of his miraculous signs, Jesus performed at Cana in Galilee. He thus revealed his glory, and his disciples put their faith in him." (Read John 2:1-11).

Why is faith such an issue? Why is it so important? Because without faith man cannot understand the things of God. *But God in His wisdom has chosen to use the Holy Spirit to make known the truth, so that everyone receives the same understanding of what God's Words mean.* "Above all, you must understand that no prophecy of Scripture came about by the prophet's own interpretation" [meaning, the prophet wrote what the Holy Spirit told him to write], (2 Peter 1:20). The most important principle in Bible study is to believe that the Holy Spirit makes truth known.

A LIFE OF FAITH

We who have faith must always consider those who have little or no faith. We must encourage them to find faith and teach them how to hold on to it. This next passage is an encouragement and may help you to understand why a life of faith is so important.

"So do not throw away your confidence; it will be richly rewarded. You need to persevere so that when you have done the will of God, you will receive what he has promised. For in just a very little while, He [Christ] who is coming will come and will not delay. But my righteous one will live by faith. And if he shrinks back, I will not be pleased with him. But we are not of those who shrink back and are destroyed, but of those who believe and are saved" (Hebrews 10:35-39).

FAITH IN JESUS IS EVERYTHING

Mathew 28:18 records Jesus saying, "... All authority in heaven and on earth has been given to me." He also said, **"I and the Father are one"** (John 10:30). God wants man to cast away all doubts through faith in His Son. Let no one deceive you with doctrine which is not of Jesus Christ. 2 John 9,10 records, "Anyone who runs ahead and does not continue in the teaching of Christ does not have God;

whoever continues in the teaching has both the Father and the Son. If anyone comes to you and does not bring this teaching, do not take him into your house or welcome him."

Religions that do not teach that Jesus is the Son of the Living God, or that He was resurrected from the dead, do not believe Christ's words. Unless anyone believes this, they have no basis for a saving faith.

JESUS ADDRESSES DOUBT

After leaving Bethany Jesus was on His way back to the city and found himself hungry. He saw a fig tree with only leaves on it, and said to the tree, "... May you never bear fruit again" (Matthew 21:19). At once, the tree withered. The disciples did not know how to respond to such a happening, and asked Jesus how the fig tree dried up so quickly. Jesus said to them, *"I tell you the truth, if you have faith and do not doubt, not only can you do what was done to the fig tree, but also you can say to this mountain, Go throw yourself into the sea, and it will be done"* (Matthew 21:21). Jesus was apparently using a hyperbole, an exaggeration to get a point across, to emphasize the power of faith, and denounce the spirit of doubting. There is a distinct difference in thinking you have faith and knowing you have a saving faith. Confessing with your mouth from the heart that Jesus Christ was raised from the dead by the power of the Holy Spirit is indeed showing a true faith, and this is a saving faith. When you tell others about Christ, your faith will grow stronger.

DOUBTING IS UNPROFITABLE

Some go through life with a certain skepticism, or doubting, which bears no profit. *Man's relationship with God is fully dependent upon faith.* This faith is centered and focused upon Jesus Christ and the Word of God, which is the Holy Bible. There is absolutely nothing on this earth, or in the heavens, or in the spirit of the individual that is apart from God. God knows all things. He is the creator and the sustainer of life. Apart From Him, we can do nothing.

TRYING TO UNDERSTAND FAITH

We express a certain kind of faith in knowing the sun will come up in the morning and the ocean tides will rise and recede. We have a certain kind of faith in our relationships and friendships. How we feel about someone is an inner experience, and telling someone what we think about them is an outward expression of our faith. 2 Corinthians 5:7 reads, "We live by faith, not by sight." *There is a vast difference in expressing a faith through physical eyes and a faith through spiritual eyes.* The faith of a baby in his mother is the kind of faith God wants us to have. Faith increases as we use our faith. Everyone who asks will receive, said Jesus in Matthew 7:8. Faith, by some, is expressed quite easily, while others give no hint about their faith.

THE PRIMACY OF FAITH
AND IT'S ACCOMPANYING ASSURANCE

Our faith is started through the Word of God and it continues to grow. Jude, one of Jesus' brothers, was concerned with those who were leaving the faith in the early church, knowing that apostasy leads to sinning. Jude urges Christians today. He said, "But you, dear friends, *build yourselves up* in your most holy faith and *pray in the Holy Spirit. Keep yourselves in God's love* as you wait for the mercy of our Lord Jesus Christ to bring you eternal life. Be merciful to those who doubt, snatch others from the fire and save them. To others, *show mercy,* mixed with fear—hating even the clothing stained by corrupted flesh. *To him who is able to keep you from falling* and to present you before his glorious presence without fault and with great joy to the only God our Savior be glory, majesty, power, and authority, through Jesus Christ our Lord, before all ages, now and forevermore! Amen" (Jude 20-25). To keep the weeds from snuffing out your faith—use it.

HEROES OF FAITH

Abel's faith won him God's approval as a man of righteousness, which is holy and upright living. Enoch's faith, which pleased God, kept him from dying. God took him into heaven and no one could find him. Without faith, Noah would not have been able to build a boat and save his family. Without faith, Abraham could not have offered up his son Isaac as a sacrifice. The faith of Moses enabled him to bring the Jews out of bondage from Egypt.

FAITH AND LIFESTYLE

Does our faith show up in our lifestyle? Yes it does show up in how we live after we have faith in Christ Jesus. As one's faith in the doctrine of Jesus Christ deepens so does his selection of many things. Closer company with like people will affect lifestyle. Church attendance will take on a deeper meaning, and a rationing of the believer's time will be directed toward things that are more beneficial. Lifestyle is a good barometer of one's faith. The deeper the faith, the deeper the burden toward the unsaved and service to God.

FAITH..... OFF AND ON!

Perhaps we take our faith for granted. Maybe we look at faith in the same way we look at electric power. We only notice it when it's out. Each one of us has a certain element of faith. To believe in man's faith and honesty is one thing, but faith in God is a whole different thing. Unless faith in God's values is lived by, then all things become worthless. We make our best decisions when we base them on the Word of God. Within the heart of the Christian, faith needs to be expressed through a personal commitment. Faith requires action.

MEASURING FAITH

Is there a way to measure faith? Here are seven actions to measure our faith.

SEVEN ACTIONS OF FAITH

1. **How we _endure_ under difficult conditions. (2 Peter 1:6,7)**

2. **How often we _pray_. (1 Thessalonians 5:17)**

3. **How often we _study_ the Word of God. (2 Timothy 2:15)**

4. **When we _live_ according to the Word of God. (John 15:7)**

5. **When we have _fellowship_ with believers. (John 17:21)**

6. **When we _witness_ with "our message" to strangers. (John 17:20)**

7. **When we _do kind acts_ and share things with others. (Acts 20:35)**

CHRISTIANS CAN'T HAVE IT BOTH WAYS

Evidence of the Christian's faith should show in his walk. If the Holy Spirit, who is given at the time of conversion, really lives in the Christian, then the Christian's birthright demands a separation from the ways of the world or doing anything which leads to immoral or ungodly behavior. The saved Christian, now having power over sin through the indwelling of the Holy Spirit, will reflect a change in lifestyle. "What shall we say, then? Shall we go on sinning so that grace may increase? By no means! We died to sin; how can we live in it any longer" (Romans 6:1,2). The Word of God is firm. Jesus said about such matters: "No servant [Christian] can serve two masters. Either he will hate the one and love the other, or he will be devoted to the one and despise the other. You cannot serve both God and mammon" (Luke 16:13).

Mammon is defined as wealth, riches, gold, or money or those things, which are worth money. These things can change the attitude and spirit of the believer toward praying, studying the Word of God, walking with God, testifying for Christ, and living charitably. Today, more so than ever, we are faced with many worldly things which take us away from God. Materialism outranks spiritualism. Christians have God's help. Believers should remember that the Holy Spirit who lives in them is greater than Satan who continues to lead them to sin. (1 John 4:4). Because the Holy Spirit lives in the believer, they have a greater advantage. *We must always look toward our faith, because it is a constant test of our love for God.*

THE POWER OF OUR FAITH
AND THE SOURCE OF THE POWER

Faith is our power source, and the Holy Spirit is the source of that power. There is a positive field of action when the two are combined. The individual's faith and the power of the Holy Spirit will do wonderful and surprising things. Faith is perfected through the action of the Christian (James 2:22). Faith, without action, is a dead faith (James 5:17). True believers and followers of Jesus, by nature of the Spirit's presence, can use their faith in everything they do. When we Christians pray, study, live the Word, have fellowship with other believers, witness, do kind acts, and endure any and all afflictions, we will know we are using the seven actions of faith. These are worth rehearsing often because the repetition of them will help perfect our walk with God.

THROUGH FAITH
THE TRULY SAVED CAN EXPECT GREAT THINGS

The person who is truly saved by God's grace and who lives with a strong working faith will live a different lifestyle. The Word of God demands a different lifestyle. *To be born of the Spirit has to be the most unique experience in a person's life.* The Bible reveals an important message on this. "Therefore, if anyone is in Christ, he is a new creation; the old has gone, the new has come!" (2 Corinthians 5:17). What are the old things? The old things represent the old sinful nature that created destruction and separation from God.

When a person is really in Christ, he will know it because things will feel new. The Spirit gives new life and we are reformed and elevated to a higher plane of living. What are these new things? The new things are those things that God the Father gives. *First*, there is the Holy Spirit of God who comes in and lives in the believer. Through His presence and power, faith is able to grow. When we ask God for knowledge and understanding He will give it. The peace, which passes all understanding, will come into the believer and a more peaceful life becomes a reality, because our dependency is no longer upon ourselves. *Secondly,* the true follower receives the fruits of the Spirit, which are love, joy, peace, faithfulness, gentleness, and goodness. It is at this point in the believer's life that he may feel the joys of his faith. These new things are better than the old things, which led us on a path to destruction. Through prayer and perseverance, a closer fellowship becomes deep-seated.

By following Christ's teachings and then adding to our faith (through our own initiative) goodness, self-control, godliness, brotherly kindness and love; our lives will take on a whole new meaning. When this happens, many will see the difference in the believer and it is this difference which makes a great testimony of what God can do when we give Him free reign in our lives. However, all of this requires the working of our faith.

The Book of James is a collection of practical instruction for the Christian. It tells about such things as riches and poverty, temptations, good conduct, *and our faith.* It directs us in the true practice of our Christian heritage. It is important to discover faith and its power. When we compare it to grace, we see two different things. Grace is given as a gift and is something we cannot add to or take away, because grace is grace. Faith is somewhat different. Mentioned earlier in this chapter, we know that faith comes from the Holy Spirit and prayer enriches our faith.

A TWOFOLD FAITH

Saving faith is what we have when we first believe. It begins the moment we believe in the gospel message of Christ (John 3:15). *Working faith* is the result of our commitment to follow after and serve our Savior Jesus Christ. Our faith is made more complete when we do something with it. However, do not consider the working of your faith as trying to repay God for your salvation through any works, because God does not allow that. We are not saved by the works we do, but by God's grace. Doing this would not be true with God's Word, and if it were a direct intent of the heart, it would minimize Christ's own personal sacrifice for you. Simply put, we have been saved by grace. It is a gift from God and we cannot work for, or boast, about what we might do (Ephesians 2:8).

GOD TESTED ABRAHAM'S FAITH

Abraham's faith was shown through his actions. His actions were working with His faith. His faith was made complete by what he did. God asked Abraham to sacrifice his son as a burnt offering. As the two of them were walking toward the designated place to make the offering, Isaac asked Abraham "... where is the lamb for the burnt offering? Abraham answered; God himself will provide the lamb for the burnt offering, my son. And the two of them went on together.

When they reached the place God had told him about, Abraham built an altar there and arranged the wood on it. He bound his son Isaac and laid him on the altar, on top of the wood. Then he reached out his hand and took the knife to slay his son. But the angel of the Lord called out to him from heaven, Abraham! Abraham! Here I am he replied. Do not lay a hand on the boy, he said. Do not do anything to him. *Now I know that you fear God*, because you have not withheld from me your son, your only son. Abraham looked up and there in a thicket he saw a ram caught by its horns. He went over, took the ram, and sacrificed it as a burnt offering instead of his son. So, Abraham called that place **The Lord Will Provide.** And to this day, it is said, "... On the mountain of the Lord it will be provided" (Genesis 22:14).

A Christian is justified by what he does and not by faith alone (James 2: 22,24). Faith is the substance of our conviction and is first expressed through our belief in Christ. It then is subject to grow into a meaningful working faith. It gets stronger as we study and apply the words of God in our attitude, behavior, and service.

The Christian's *working faith* keeps him busy in doing the works which any true Christian will do. Working faith is the result of the believer's daily commitment to serve God according to the Word of God. Because we are believers, we must remember the very most important role that our faith plays in our Christian walk. We are never to take our eyes off Christ Jesus. Abraham did not relax his faith in God. Christians today keep their faith in God through Christ.

PETER'S FAITH WAS TESTED

Peter, when he tried to walk on the water, took his eyes off Jesus the minute a little wind distracted him. But Jesus reached out and saved him. Then Jesus said to him, "You of little faith, why did you doubt?" (Read Matthew 14:28-31).

The Christian challenge is to think and act by faith, knowing that Jesus lives in them through the presence of the Holy Spirit. *Faith, when coupled with action is a working faith, and if we have faith, we cease to doubt.*

WE LEARN FROM JESUS' MIRACLES

Let us look into the account of Jesus when He fed the five thousand and what it was that He said to them. From the book of John, we review the very important words of Jesus, as it relates to our personal faith in Him.

A crowd of people sought out Jesus, after He had fed them with only five loaves of bread and two small fish. Jesus knew they were trying to find Him, and said to them, "I tell you the truth, you are looking for me, not because you saw miraculous signs but because you ate the loaves and had your fill. *Do not work for food that spoils, but for food that endures to eternal life, which the Son of Man will give you...*" (John 6: 26-27).

Jesus was able to see through their intention. The purpose for the miracle was to give the Israelites (Jews) the opportunity to see that this man Jesus was really who He says He was — the promised Messiah. The Jews could not see the miracles, which Jesus performed, as any proof of His deity and purpose. Most people today see no better, even when they are told that the Bible contains the message of salvation. They still refuse to answer the call of our almighty God. The words of Christ, "Do not work for food that spoils," refers to anyone doing things which lead them to fill their spiritual appetites with the wrong bread. Jesus said that He is the bread of life and Apart From Him, man cannot receive the blessings of God. However, if, you are touched enough in your faith to believe in what Jesus was saying, then you should know that there are certain things which must be done, that is, if you believe in the written Word of God. Here are some of those things that have been written and must be done.

(1) Come to Christ. ".... Whoever comes to me I will never drive away". (John 6:37)
(2) "Obey the commandments". (Matthew 19:17)
(3) If you have been set free from sin, then live that way. (Romans 6:18)
(4) Sow to please the Holy Spirit . (Galatians 6:8)
(5) "Fight the good fight of the faith". (1 Timothy 6:12)

(6) Learn to overcome temptations. (James 1:12)
(7) Love everyone. (1 John 3:14)

Obviously, Jesus is talking about working for spiritual food which comes through faith and obedience. It does require work, and it is the kind of work which will last. The Bible says, "Live as free men, but do not use your freedom as a cover-up for evil; live as servants of God. Show proper respect to everyone: Love the brotherhood of believers, fear God, honor the king" (1 Peter 2:16,17).

CHRISTIANS UNDER GRACE

Christians because they are under grace must not think there is nothing more to do. Jesus set the record straight to the question of "What must we do to do the works God requires?" Jesus said, "The work of God is this: to believe in the one he has sent" (John 6:29).

Jesus is everything the Christian needs to sustain himself under any condition. *The main thing is to continue to believe in Christ through a sincere and deep commitment, which can only be accomplished through faith and obedience to the Word of God.* We know that believing is the result of our faith. Jesus' saying, "He who comes to me" was not to be taken as a one time gesture of good intention, and then riding out the rest of our Christian experience without following His teachings. Until anyone comes to Christ and is converted, they cannot live under the covering of God's grace.

JESUS THE BREAD OF LIFE

"**J**esus declared, I am the bread of life. *He who comes to me* will never go hungry, and *he who believes in me* will never be thirsty. But as I told you, you have seen me and still you do not believe" (John 6:35-36). We cannot see Jesus with our physical eyes as the Jews and His disciples did in their time. Anyone, today, can see Him through their spiritual eyes, if they are open. This kind of sight is made complete through faith.

FAITH AND ITS RELATIONSHIP
TO THE BELIEVER'S MARRIAGE TO CHRIST

Faith through obedience in any marriage provides a strong bond.

68

Marriage (a mutual relation of husband and wife) is a full time relationship with continuous commitment. The Scriptures use the word "marriage" to help us understand more intimately the relationship of the believer and Christ.

Jesus, who is depicted as the groom and the body of believers, are depicted as the bride of Christ, are one in a marriage. This is what Jesus was talking about in Matthew 22:4 when He said "... Come to the wedding banquet." He was teaching and preparing us for the marriage He had in mind, which would be taking place after His sacrifice for the sins of the world.

The wedding of the Lamb is mentioned in Revelation 19:7. Symbolically, this refers to Christ's coming for his believers. It gives us insight into the relationship or alliance that exists between Christ and His body of believers. It reads "Let us rejoice and be glad and give him glory! For the wedding of the Lamb has come, and his bride has made herself ready. Fine linen, bright and clean was given her to wear." (Fine linen stands for the righteous acts of the saints).

The groom, who is Christ, will be returning for His bride, the Church. They are the redeemed of all ages. Jesus called himself the **bridegroom** in Matthew 9:15. This is when He said, "The time will come when the **bridegroom** will be taken from them; then they will fast." Jesus (The bridegroom) was taken up to heaven after His resurrection. What did Jesus mean when He said, "they will fast?" We know that a deeper and richer faith is developed through prayer and fasting in secret. Fasting, though not embraced, is practiced by some Christians.

LEAVING THE FAITH—A SERIOUS WARNING

Paul sends a strong message to the brethren when he says, "See to it, brothers, that none of you has a sinful, unbelieving heart that *turns away* from the living God" (Hebrews 3:12). What a contrast we have as we re-read this next passage. "Therefore, if anyone is in Christ, he is a new creation; the old has gone, the new has come!" (2 Corinthians 5:17). Paul doesn't say when you are in Christ, he says if you are in Christ. Faith is the stimulus of Christianity. Satan is still roaming the fields of this earth and trying to undo the faith of many. Can one's faith be given up or abandoned? Paul instructed Timothy to "Fight the good fight of the faith. Take hold of the eternal life to which you were called when you made your good confession in the presence of many witnesses" This is when a saving faith is openly expressed in Christ (1 Timothy 6:12). *From this we know that we must not slip backward*, just move ahead. We must be very determined in our pursuit and aggressively follow the role of Christ-like behavior.

Keeping the faith demands full commitment, as we will see in this next passage. Paul said, "I have fought the good fight, I have finished the race, I have kept the faith" (2 Timothy 4:7).

Paul tells the converted Jews. "See to it, brothers, that none of you has a sinful heart that *turns away* from the living God" (Hebrews 3:12). Paul further identifies the brethren as Christians when he said, "We have come to share in Christ if we hold firmly till the end the confidence we had at first" (Hebrews 3:14). Peter credits Paul with writing to the Jews, which is who the book of Hebrews is addressed to. Here's what Peter said, "... just as our dear brother Paul also wrote you with the wisdom that God gave him" (2 Peter 3:15). Paul's words, "turn away", and "if we hold firmly" should put us on notice to persevere with deep conviction through faith.

Things to do to help you keep the faith:

(1) Encourage other Christians daily. (Hebrews. 3:13)
(2) Hold firmly to your faith. (Hebrews. 4:14)
(3) Hold on to your courage and hope. (Hebrews. 3:6)
(4) Watch your life and doctrine closely. (1 Tim. 4:16)
(5) Do everything in love. (Galatians 5:6)
(6) Be in control of your life. (2 Peter 1:6)
(7) Watch and pray to keep temptation away.
  (Matthew 26:41)

Things not to do:

(1) Do not be lazy in your Christian life. (Hebrews. 6:12)
(2) Keep from any and all sins. (Hebrews. 10:26)
(3) Don't join others who do sinful things. (2 Peter 3:17)
(4) Stay away from false religions. (2 Peter 2:1)
(5) Don't throw away your confidence. (Hebrews. 10:35)

(6) See to it that you do not refuse God. (Hebrews 12:25)

(7) Keep your distance from anything immoral.
(Romans 2:8)

UNWAVERING FAITH

A centurion came to Jesus, asking for help.... "Lord, he said, my servant lies at home paralyzed and in terrible suffering. Jesus said I will go and heal him. The centurion replied, Lord I do not deserve to have you come under my roof. But *just say the word*, and my servant will be healed. When Jesus heard this, he was astonished and said to those following him, I tell you the truth, I have not found anyone in Israel with such great faith" (Matthew 8:5-8, 10). The centurion had absolute dependence and confidence in Christ Jesus. Can we have this kind of unquestionable faith today? Yes, we can. We must, though, trust wholly and unreservedly in the faithfulness of God. Faith comes to us when we listen to, and hear the Word of God. *Obedience is the bond of our faith.* We know that we are living in difficult times. We are seeing more filth and decay in our society than ever before. Now is the time to take an inventory of our spiritual assets, find out our weak spots, and develop them into strengths. The important thing is to ask God for increased faith, wisdom, and then leave it up to Him to deliver. We know that, "... if we ask according to His will, he hears us. And if we know that he hears us—whatever we ask—we know that we have what we asked of him" (1 John 5:14-15).

"The Spirit clearly says that in the later times some will abandon the faith and follow deceiving spirits and things taught by demons" (1 Timothy 4:1). Remaining true to God is vital, if, we want to win the race.

Jesus said, "Not everyone who says to me, Lord, Lord, will enter the kingdom of heaven, *but only he who does the will of my Father* who is in heaven. Many will say to me on that day, Lord, Lord, did we not prophecy in your name, and in your name drive out demons and perform many miracles? Then I will tell them plainly, I never knew you. Away from me, you evil doers" (Matthew 7: 21-23). Ask God for faith and you will get it.

71

DRAWING ON THE FULL ASSURANCE OF FAITH

"Therefore, brothers, since we have confidence to enter the Most Holy Place by the blood of Jesus, [meaning direct access to God] by a new and living way opened for us through the curtain, that is his body, and since we have a great priest [Jesus Christ] over the House of God, let us draw near to God with a sincere heart in full assurance of faith, having our hearts sprinkled to cleanse us from a guilty conscience and having our bodies washed with pure water [meaning our spiritual baptism into Christ]. Let us hold unswervingly to the hope we profess, for he who promised is faithful. And let us consider how we may spur one another on toward love and good deeds. Let us not give up meeting together, as some are in the habit of doing, but let us encourage one another—and all the more as you see the Day approaching" (Hebrews 10: 19-25).

Faith, in theological perspective, is being sure of things we do not see. It is accepting and believing the Word of God as certain, true and good. It is not relying upon logical proof. Faith is private. It is necessary to come into a relationship with God, through Christ. It is a prime requisite to salvation. It is not something that can be legislated, or agreed upon, as in concert with others. Faith is personal. Faith, in and through the Holy Spirit holds us together in Jesus Christ. Faith in Christ is the most precious asset a person can possess. Faith, and only faith, moves us toward the Glory of God. Faith, as a theological virtue is our security anchor to the Son of the Living God, Jesus Christ. Faith comes when your hear and receive the Holy Word of God.

Faith is a gift that comes from the precious Grace of God

CHAPTER 7

GOD'S PLAN OF SALVATION

What is God's plan of salvation? It is God's instrument of restoring man from sin and destruction. His plan to bring man to Himself continues because of His great mercy and grace. "But the Scripture declares that the whole world is a prisoner of sin, so that what was promised [restoration and healing], being given through faith in Jesus Christ, might be given to those who believe" (Galatians 3:22). The promise mentioned here by Paul refers to what Isaiah the prophet wrote concerning the coming of Christ the Savior of the world. "But he was pierced for our transgressions, he was crushed for our iniquities; the punishment that brought us peace was upon him, and by his wounds we are healed" (Isaiah 53:5).

What is the significance of salvation? Without it, there is no redemption. "Our God is a God who saves; from the Sovereign Lord comes escape from death" (Psalms 68:20). It is very important for man to come to know that his state before God is sin stained. "The Lord saw how great man's wickedness on the earth had become, and that every inclination of the thoughts of his heart was only evil all the time" (Genesis 6:5).

Why is salvation such an important part of Christianity? *We are first saved by God's grace through our faith, then we become Christians*. Christians are those who trust, follow, and obey Christ's teachings. We do not become good then find God. He takes us as we are. Man cannot have a right relationship with God until he comes to know Christ.

GOD RECONCILES US FOR HIS OWN PURPOSE

"I, even I, am he who blots out your transgressions, for my own sake, and remembers your sins no more" (Isaiah 43:25). God did not spare the ungodly at the time of the great flood, but saved Noah and the seven members of his godly family. This is evidence that God wants to save and restore man (2 Peter 2:5). If it were not for Noah, man might not have had a second chance.

Man is foolish in the sight of God. Selfishness, greed, idolatry, sexual desire with a degrading passion, and evil can be reversed. Man must come back to God. What can justify man before God? Believing in the resurrected Christ will justify man before God. God sees the wickedness in man today in the same way He has all through the centuries; man is a helpless creature and unless he reaches to the one who saves, he is doomed to hell. Man needs to be rescued from his condition of sin and rebellion. Apart from Christ, he cannot do it. Throughout the ages, God has punished man for his disobedience. How much longer will God put up with our stubbornness? Only God knows that.

GOD WANTS MAN FOR HIMSELF—SINLESS

All through history, man has proven his sinful and evil behavior before a patient God. God wants man to be delivered from sin. Why? Because He loves all people and wants them to come back to Him, without sin. Through Jesus Christ, God makes this possible. He provides no other way. It is only through Jesus Christ that man can be redeemed or recovered. Only through believing in the cross of Christ and His resurrection can man be forgiven, and come into the grace of God. God's Word was written for this purpose. It contains the message of hope; it delivers the only doctrine that can save man from hell. This doctrine is the doctrine of Jesus Christ. It is permanent, forever, never ending. It is God's grace.

WHY IS IT IMPORTANT FOR US TO HEED GOD'S WARNING?

Jesus, when He was talking to His disciples about His coming rejection and suffering, referred to the times of Lot and Noah. He reminded them of violent behavior, and how God had sent sudden destruction upon the cities of Sodom and Gomorrah because of their deep sinning. Jesus compared the swiftness of God's destruction of these two cities to His returning in the coming ending times. *He further warned against having false security in the things of this world.* When Jesus returns for His believers, there will be no time for anyone to prepare or be sorry. It will be too late. Will you be left behind? (Read Luke 17:26-33). What is your position on these things? Why not come to know and believe in God's plan of salvation. It is

His almighty plan to restore you into His family. Because God loves us so much, He sent His only Son to suffer and die for our sins (John 3:16). God is Spirit (John 4:24), and He has provided but one means for spiritual restoration and that means is Jesus Christ (John 18:37). *God wants everyone to be with Him forever, on His terms.* Though salvation itself requires faith, repentance, commitment, and obedience, the Christian must follow those things that have been handed down through the apostles and the prophets. *First,* there must be a washing away of our sins, which is why Jesus died. "He saved us, not because of righteous things we had done, but because of his mercy. He saved us through the washing of rebirth and renewal by the Holy Spirit whom he poured out on us generously through Jesus Christ our Savior, so that, **having been justified by his grace**, we might become heirs having the hope of eternal life" (Titus 3: 5-7). *Secondly,* there must be a determination to live morally, make amends, and correction to lifestyle. All worldly pleasures and old sinful possessions must be given up and trashed. The Holy Spirit will help you if He does indeed live in you (Romans 8:8). *Thirdly,* true Christian living is encompassed in trusting, following, and obeying the teachings of Christ. To those who may not yet be saved, this may look like a pretty tall order. However, those who have sincerely and truthfully made their commitment to Christ, living up to God's expectations, will tell you how better off they are, compared to their old life.

BELIEVERS ARE GIVEN POWER AND ASSURANCE FROM ABOVE

At the specific time of a person's conversion, God pours His Holy Spirit into them. The believer receives the "gift of the Holy Spirit" as they surrender their life to and receive Christ as Savior and Lord (Acts 2:38). From this point forward, the true believer is no longer apart from God. They are provided with God's power. "You, however, are controlled not by the sinful nature but by the Spirit, if the Spirit of God lives in you" (Romans 8:9). The conjunction "if" should place deep concern in the hearts of those who may not be certain of their position in Christ. God has a plan for everyone's salvation. The question is— are we meeting His requirements?

Here's a way to check yourself .

(1) *Have you really come to Christ with a full commitment?* "All that the Father gives me will come to me, and whoever comes to me I will never drive away" (John 6:37).

(2) *How real is your belief in His resurrection and have you truly made an open confession of Jesus Christ to God?* "That if you confess with your mouth, Jesus is Lord, and believe in your heart that God raised him from the dead, you will be saved" (Romans 10:9).

(3) *Do you know God and Christ?* "Now this is eternal life: that they may know you, the only true God, and Jesus Christ, whom you have sent" (John 17:3).

(4) *Have you entered the right gate of life?* "Enter through the narrow gate. For wide is the gate and broad is the road that leads to destruction, and many enter through it. But small is the gate and narrow is the road that leads to life, and only a few find it" (Matthew 7:13-14).

(5) *Do you keep His commandments?* "Those who obey his commands live in him, and he in them. And this is how we know that he lives in us: We know it by the Spirit he gave us" (1 John 3:24).

(6) *Is Christ the center of your life?* "See that what you have heard from the beginning remains in you. If it does, you also will remain in the Son and in the Father. And this is what he promised us—eternal life" (1 John 2:24-25).

(7) *How truly obedient are you to the laws of God?* Faith in evidence is obedience in evidence (Romans 1:5). "... and we take captive every thought to make it obedient to Christ" (2 Corinthians 10:5).

LIVING BY ONE OF TWO NATURES

When you read this next passage please observe Paul's use of the word "if". Paul, addressing believers, said this. "Therefore, *brothers,*

76

we have an obligation—but it is not to the sinful nature, to live according to it. For if you live according to the sinful nature, you will die; *but if by the Spirit you put to death the misdeeds of the body,* you will live, because those who are led by the Spirit of God are the sons of God, For you did not receive a spirit that makes you a slave to fear, but you received the Spirit of sonship. And by him we cry, Abba, Father. The Spirit himself testifies with our spirit that we are God's children" (Romans 8: 12-16). Here we see that God has given us His own presence that we may be able to fight victoriously against the temptations of life.

Does the Spirit of God live in you? If He does, then, you can expect great victory. If He does not, then we know we can do nothing on our own. When we have Jesus, we have the Spirit. Jesus said, without me you can do nothing.

JESUS FULFILLS SCRIPTURE AND ITS MEANING

These next events took place just prior to Christ's death. "Later, knowing that all was now completed, and so that the scripture would be fulfilled, Jesus said, I am thirsty. A jar of wine vinegar was there, so they soaked a sponge in it, put the sponge on a stalk of the hyssop plant, and lifted it to Jesus' lips. When he had received the drink, Jesus said, It is finished. With that, he bowed his head and gave up his spirit" (John 19: 28-30).

The significance of the final three words of Christ "It is finished" should bring shouts of joy in the hearts of all believers. They represent Christ's victory over Satan and the completion of His work. They mean:

(1) Scripture was fulfilled (Isaiah 53).
(2) Satan was defeated (John 12:31-32).
(3) Jews and Gentiles could now be one in Christ (Ephesians 2:14-18).
(4) A personal and direct access to God is now possible (Hebrews 10: 19-25).
(5) Man can now escape God's judgment (Romans 8:1-2).
(6) "Death has been swallowed up in victory" (1 Corinthians 15:54).

(7) Jesus set the example of our obedience. He was obedient until He died (Philippians 2:8).

(8) A finished and completed work which will never again be repeated (Hebrews 10:12).

If you cannot say, for certain, that you are saved, then why not ask Christ Jesus into your life? Do you believe the final words of Jesus "It is finished"? Do you think anything else can be added to God's holy work? The believer is given special help to grow according to the written Word of God. John 14:26 tells us that the Holy Spirit will teach us all things. Temptation is still present, but we are given God's Spirit to help us. The unsaved do not have God's Spirit, as there must first be a conversion. This conversion brings about a change.

Believers, according to 1 John 5:20, know they belong to God. They also know and believe that the world they live in is under the rule of Satan. They also know that because God's Spirit lives in them, they have a better chance to survive the wickedness in this world.

ONCE FORGIVEN NEVER TO BE REMEMBERED

Who can question the God of life and all creation? God is pure and holy. He cannot and will not associate with sin. He makes this very plain in the Scriptures. He makes us His children, for Himself, and for His own purpose. When we receive Christ as our Savior, we become His children. He makes us perfect according to His purpose. He does this because He loves us so very much. That is why He said, *"For my own sake I will not remember your sins."* We can relate to a mother's love. By virtue of her love, a normal and loving mother will never let go of her child.

FORGIVENESS AND JUDGMENT

According to the written Word of God, forgiveness is a vital part of God's plan of salvation. If He would not forgive and forget (because one is not possible without the other), there would be no full and complete pardon for our sins. With pardon, there is no judgment. Roman 8:1 records, "Therefore, there is now no condemnation [judgment] for those who are in Christ Jesus..." John 3:18 says, "Whoever believes in him is not condemned, but who ever does not believe stands condemned already because he has not believed in the name of God's one and only Son."

Does God remember our sins? Hebrews 10:17 says, "... Their sins and lawless acts I will remember no more. And where these have been forgiven, there is no longer any sacrifice for sin."

GOD'S PROMISE TO THOSE WHO WILL BELIEVE

Jesus said, "I tell you the truth, whoever hears my word and believes him who sent me has eternal life and will not be condemned; he has crossed over from death to life" (John 5:24). *The person who believes in Christ will never be separated from God, Jesus, and the Holy Spirit.*

This is God's plan of salvation—while man could do nothing to save himself, God could. *Nothing can be added to what Christ did at the cross.* Jesus did it all. Works cannot improve what God has made perfect.

The believer is no longer separated from God, because he believed upon Christ. He now has God the Father and the Son (2nd John 9). He is now in the family of God. It is foolish to think otherwise when the Word of God is so clear. Jesus uses the word "believe" very often; He does not say understand or add anything. While it is very difficult to comprehend such deep mysteries, Jesus merely asks us to believe. If we truly believe, we will surely take action that will result into a saving faith. He also compared faith to a mustard seed: "... If you have faith as small as a mustard seed..." (Matthew 17:20). Jesus used this parable to show what even a small amount of faith can do for anyone who is ready to follow Him.

WHAT IS YOUR ANSWER TO GOD'S CALL?
HAVE YOU BEEN BORN AGAIN?

There can be only one of two answers to the latter question. It is either "yes" or "no." There is no such thing as perhaps, maybe, I think so, I belong to a Christian church, I'm a good giver, I work in the church, or I read the Bible. Don't be fooled by such notions. Salvation is not possible through works or goodness. Salvation is a gift from God and is available through faith. Jesus said, "Because you have seen me, you have believed, *blessed are those who have not seen and yet have believed"* (John 20:29).

FACING A PARDON

I have known men in prisons who would give anything for a pardon. Some of these men actually become obsessed with the notion that something will happen, and they will get a pardon. Why is this? Well, for one reason, they have had their freedom removed. They no longer govern their own lives. Who is governing your life? *Truth sets the believer free because Jesus is the truth.* Prisoners are separated from society just as the sinner is separated from God until the time a pardon is granted. What ever you may be a prisoner to, remember this, Jesus can take you out of any situation.

HOW DO YOU GET A PARDON?

The Lord said, "Let the wicked forsake his way and the evil man his thoughts. Let him turn to the Lord, and he will have mercy on him, and to our God, **for he will freely pardon**" (Isaiah 55:7).

The person who is ignorant about the necessity of a pardon for his sins falls into one of several categories:

(1)   He has not read or studied the Holy Bible, or is filled with pride and cannot conceive forgiveness.
(2)   He is hardened by sin and blind to the mercy of God.
(3)   He is unenlightened about the need for God's pardon.
(4)   He thinks the "all have sinned" Bible verse is just religious talk, and the church will get him to heaven.
       Have you been pardoned for your sins? The believer says, yes.

ARROGANCE COULD COST YOU YOUR LIFE

Are you one of those who think God is love, and He will not do all of those things He says He will do to the unsaved, such as sending them to hell to suffer in torment forever? The Bible tells us it will be either heaven or hell. Revelation 20:15 records, "If anyone's name was not found written in the book of life, he was thrown into the lake of fire." This is Hell, or Gehenna. Those who come from religious backgrounds and are not grounded in truth are the targeted people of

GOD'S PLAN OF SALVATION

false religions. False religions paint a far different picture than that which is given to us in the Holy Scriptures. Jesus is our only hope. Check it out for yourself; the benefits are out of this world.

COMING TO KNOW ABOUT THE BOOK OF LIFE?

The Book of Life holds the names of everyone who believed in what Jesus said of Himself in John 6:38, "For I have come down from heaven not to do my will but to do the will of him who sent me." The will of the Father is that all people be saved and come into the knowledge of truth (1 Timothy 2:4). Jesus fulfilled God's will so that those who come to Him can have life eternal.

The Book of Life is God's record of those who are covered under the Blood of the Lamb. Jesus is that Lamb and is the only way to God; there is no other way. Daniel the prophet brought this up (12:1) six hundred and seven plus years BC. "... But at that time your people—everyone whose name is found written in the book—will be delivered."

If anyone rejects God's plan of salvation, they should know what they are in for and hear what He is saying. "May they be blotted out of the book of life and not be listed with the righteous" (Psalms 69:28). So, it was the righteous whom God had already written into the Book of Life. If you want something to move your spirit, to shake you up, ask yourself this next question and let truth overtake you. Why haven't I really surrendered my life to Christ? According to the Scriptures, there will come a time when people will be disappointed in finding out their names were not written into the Book of Life. Unfortunately, it will be too late to do anything about it. What will you be expecting? The final judgment will be given by Jesus Christ who said, "Moreover, the Father judges no one, but has entrusted all judgment to the Son, that all may honor the Son just as they honor the Father. He who does not honor the Son does not honor the Father, who sent him" (John 5:22). You cannot have one without the other.

JESUS WILL PROCLAIM HIS OWN BEFORE THE FATHER

Recorded in Revelation 3:5, Jesus tells the apostle John, "He who overcomes will, like them, be dressed in white. I will never blot out his name from the book of life, but will acknowledge his name before my Father and his angels." To overcome means to have conquered sin, and to have overpowered our lost state through the shed Blood of Christ. To overcome means we have crushed, defeated, and conquered sin in our lives. This is accomplished only through the shed blood of Christ. He gives us His Holy Spirit to help us live godly lives. *A person who is truly saved will remain obedient to the laws of God, even as Christ was obedient unto His death.*

PRACTICAL CONSIDERATIONS

When we come to think upon these things—living, dying, salvation, and judgment—which have been written for our use, we must come to God as a little child and ask for His help. *No one really wants to make the wrong choice. Because it is your life which hangs in the balance,* why should you not be more objective? Do you really know if you are truly saved? Here is why this question is so important. Many people profess Christianity and they may have been brought up in a Christian church, or they may have been practicing some other religion, but they have not yet come to grips with the true meaning of God's plan of salvation.

If you have not repented, and have not given your life to Christ, then where do you think you fit in God's plan of salvation? Jesus said, "I tell you, No! But unless you repent, you too will all perish" (Luke 13:5). If you have not, then why not accept Christ into your life now? When could there be a better time to make your peace with God?

God's love for man is hard to understand. God is love and man can only learn to love. So, man's love is conditional. God's love is never ending. Man's life is governed by his moods and his temperament. Stepping out in faith will override these things and great changes will occur. When an individual comes to Jesus Christ, believes upon Him, and accepts Him as the Savior of his life, he receives the gift of life and the gift of the Holy Spirit (Acts 2:38). Good works does not precede salvation because we are saved by grace. No one is saved by good works such as acts of kindness, financial giving to the church, or working with church committees. It is only after we have committed ourselves to Christ that we can walk in obedience through the Holy

Spirit.

NEW STANDARD TO LOVE AND LIVE BY

New converts first receive the gift of the Holy Spirit and then learn to live and love by a different standard. The new standard of love brings with it a spirit of giving and forgiving. *It is good to remember "the law of love" is forgiveness.* No forgiveness, no love. The old standard of love was selfish, and too often, we thought in terms of a tradeoff. Think, if you will, upon what this next passage is saying. "As for you, the anointing you received from him [Holy Spirit] remains in you, and you do not need anyone to teach you. But as his [Holy Spirit's] anointing teaches you about all things and as that anointing is real, not counterfeit—just as it has taught you, remain in him" (1 John 2:27). To remain in Him means we draw upon His presence and do all things, through Him, with the same obedient nature He had.

Because we believe, we are given a confidence in everything we do. A small example of this may be explained, and understood better, as we think upon how our confidence level shoots up when someone believes in us and trusts us. I always do so much better when I know that someone has placed confidence in me; it stirs me. How much more should we be stirred, knowing, that God's Holy Spirit has come into us?

THE BELIEVER'S GAIN

The apostle Peter gives us this very important message. Those who believe upon Jesus are born again, born of God, and born into the family of God through the enduring word of God (1 Peter 1:23). He further assures us of the seed by which we are born. He speaks about an incorruptible seed. This seed comes from the Word of God, through the Holy Spirit of God. He is talking about God, who is immortal. Through this incorruptible seed, the body of believers have become His children. *Believers who trust Christ will obey Christ.*

THE GOOD NEWS ABOUT JESUS CHRIST
GIVEN TO ALL NATIONS

The eternal plan of God according to these next two verses is certainly good news. Paul tells us in Romans 16:25,26, "Now to him [Jesus] who is able to establish you by my gospel and the proclamation of Jesus Christ, according to the revelation of the mystery hidden for long ages past, but now revealed and made known through prophetic writings by command of the eternal God, so that all nations might believe and *obey* him to the only wise God be glory forever through Jesus Christ! Amen." What a setting that must have been. Rome had a mixture of Jews, Gentiles, slaves, and many world travelers. Paul made this proclamation about Jesus, as having been made known in their times. Here we are today some two thousand years later, only to find that the Gospel of Jesus Christ is still a mystery to many people in this world. How fortunate for everyone, we are living in a period of grace. There is still time to take advantage of the greatest opportunity ever made available to mankind, the grace of God.

Have you taken advantage of God's call? This opportunity is just as authentic today as it was when Paul first preached it. Think of it! When you become a child of God, God will not give you up. Jesus said in John 6:37, "All that the Father gives me will come to me, *and whoever comes to me I will never drive away.*" Keep in mind these are the direct Words of God and not of man. I hope you will be as touched, as I was when I discovered that God's plan of salvation through His only Son, a mystery hidden from ages and generations, was now made open and available to all who could believe. I was blind to these things until the day of my salvation just twenty three years ago. Yes, joyfully, do I tell you about my hope in the Son of the Living God, Jesus Christ.

Paul told the Ephesians (1:9), "And he made known to us the mystery of his will according to his good pleasure, which he purposed in Christ." Why does God say the mystery of His will? *We must acknowledge the Sovereignty of God. His grand plan of salvation through His incarnate Son Jesus Christ is His alone.* Beyond man's measure or comprehension, God, in His infinite wisdom alone, has provided a means for man to be reconciled to Himself. *Believing upon Christ's birth, death and resurrection is that means.* According to His Holy Word there is no other way. Christ is the answer.

SALVATION IS NOT A COMPLICATED RELIGIOUS ACT

Through confessing with the mouth before God, that Jesus was raised from the dead, salvation is made easy and practicable. Romans 10:10 reads, "For it is with your heart that you believe and are justified, and it is with your mouth that you confess and are saved." God has made this possible. Paul further told the Ephesians, "To be put into effect when the times have reached their fulfillment—to bring all things in heaven and on earth together under one head, even Christ" (Ephesians 1:10).

According to this, then, it is in God's good timing that we are privileged to be living in a time of Grace.

OLD TESTAMENT DISCLOSURES

God is meticulous when it comes to His planning each and every event concerning His blueprint for man's heavenly preservation. Let us consider the following.

(1) In the first book of the Bible, Genesis 3:15, God announced the coming of Christ.

(2) In the last book in the Old Testament, Malachi 3:1, God describes the coming of John the Baptist, the man who would precede Jesus and prepare the way for Him. He also announced Jesus, who would come to His temple (397 years BC).

(3) In Isaiah 9:6 God described how Jesus would come. This was seven hundred plus years before Christ came.

(4) In Isaiah 35:5,6 God said Jesus would heal the sick, and open the eyes of the blind.

(5) In Isaiah 53:3,5 God described how Jesus would suffer to save man from hell.

(6) In Isaiah, 40:3 God announced the coming of the one who would prepare the way for Jesus; this was John the Baptist.

NEW TESTAMENT FULFILLMENT

(1) In 1 Timothy, 2:4 God says that He wants all men to be saved and come into the knowledge of truth.

(2) In Ephesians 2: 5,8 God says that we are saved by grace through faith.

(3) In 2 Timothy 1:9 God says that He had called us to His own purpose and grace through Christ Jesus, before the world began.

(4) In 2 Corinthians 5:5 God says that He wants us to know that we have life eternal.

(5) In John 10:28 Jesus says, "And I give them eternal life; and they shall never perish, neither shall any man pluck them out of my hand."

(6) In John 17:4 Jesus says, "I have brought you glory on earth by completing the work you gave me to do."

SALVATION—IS IT FOR EVERYONE?

Yes, it is for everyone, no matter who they are or what they have done with their lives. God hates all our sins and is willing, as our loving God, to forgive us. Yes, confessing and repenting people—be they cowards, liars, traitors, perverts, murderers, rapists, those who take part in occult practices, such as fortune telling and witchcraft, or those who worship idols—have a chance with God. His plan is real and alive. A person is dead in his sins before God until he comes to the only one who can do something about it, that someone is Jesus Christ, the only Savior of the world.

GOD'S ARMS ARE ALWAYS OPEN

God is just and loving. He has a place of distinction for all who will confess His Son. If God had any hate in him, or if He had a vindictive nature, we would all be burned in the Lake of Fire. It is impossible to understand the deep mysteries of God. He takes those who have dropped to a low status in life and makes something of them. The apostle Paul was bringing suffering and strife to the

Christians of that day. He was stopped by Jesus in the middle of his journey, toward Damascus. Jesus called Paul to serve Him. Paul was made blind by God for a short time, then later was healed. He went on to serve the Lord Jesus Christ with a fervent passion and dedication to his very end. Do not be surprised when you see someone with a shady past serving God today. God continues to call upon those whom He chooses to do His work.

THE UNLIMITED MERCY OF OUR LORD JESUS

The love of Jesus Christ is somewhat overwhelming. Listen to what He said in Matthew 11:28: "Come to me, all you who are weary and burdened, and I will give you rest." For the person who may be experiencing a heavy burden, this passage is always a welcome reminder of our loving Lord. Burdened here refers to someone carrying a big, unnecessary load. This passage is also calling the person who is involved in continuing deep sin: drugs, homosexuality, perversion, murder, rape, child abuse, wife beating and drunkenness. In any case, the Lord Jesus is always open to the caller. Pride and stubbornness separate man from God.

If you have not in times past placed any importance upon the idea of your salvation, make a move today. If by some chance your situation has been neglectful to these things, won't you consider taking the time right now to make a full confession before God and ask Him into to your life? *He never turns down a truly repentant person.* The call of Jesus is clear, "Come to me, all of you, who are in trouble, beaten down, and exhausted from the sins in your life. I will take you as you are, heal your life, make it whole again, and make it perfect before the Father" (The writer's words) see Matthew 11: 28-29.

POSTERITY AND THE GREAT COMMISSION

Jesus said, "... All authority in heaven and on earth has been given to me. Therefore go and make disciples of all nations, baptizing them in the name of the Father and of the Son and of the Holy Spirit" (Matthew 28:18,19). The disciples immediately began to convert people to Christianity. Then those who became believers did the same thing. They went out and became soul winners. *Believers of tomorrow are dependent upon the action of believers of today.* God is depending upon His faithful family to bring the Gospel message of Jesus Christ to the lost. "You will be his witnesses to all men of what you have seen and heard" (Acts 22:15).

BELIEVERS HAVE THEIR WORK CUT OUT FOR THEM

"Therefore, if anyone is in Christ, he is a new creation; the old has gone the new has come! All this is from God, who reconciled us to himself through Christ and gave us the *ministry* of reconciliation: that God was reconciling the world to himself in Christ, not counting men's sins against them. And he has committed to us the *message* of reconciliation" (2 Corinthians 5:17-18). What more can we say. God's word does not lie. The "message" is the Gospel of Christ. God. having reconciled [restored to harmony with Himself] man to Himself, gives the new believer authority to help others to do the same. When should a new believer do this? The Holy Bible tells us, ".... I tell you now is the time of God's favor, now is the day of salvation" (2 Corinthians 6:2).

God commands us to love Him with all of our heart and with all of our soul, and with all of our strength, and that we are to serve him in this same way. God tells us to pass these commands to our children. He wants us to talk about these things in our homes and when we are in the presence of others. (Deuteronomy 6:4-9, 10: 12-13).

Jesus says, " All that the Father gives me will come to me, and whoever comes to me I will never drive away" (John 6:37). There is only one way to God and it is through the person of Jesus Christ, who said, " I am the Alpha and the Omega, says the Lord God, who is, and who was, and is to come, the Almighty" (Revelation 1:8).

God's plan of salvation was made known through the prophets, fulfilled by Jesus Christ, carried on by the disciples, and now rests in the hands of every Christian in the world. May God guide us into greater works.

"For the grace of God that brings salvation has appeared to all men" (Titus 2: 11).

CHAPTER 8

REPENTANCE AND BAPTISM

Repentance and baptism go together. *There can be no genuine baptism without repentance.* Turning back to God and turning away from sin is a pre-requisite to baptism. Repentance should not be construed as an act of perfectibility but, rather, intent to turn away from sin. If man had to become perfect on his own prior to baptism and salvation, no one could be saved. It is always good to remember that the fruit of repentance follows a true repentance. The fruit of repentance is an inner joy of knowing that no longer are you a slave to the old sinful way of life. Eternal life now lies ahead (Romans 6:22). Repentance is the beginning of a new way of life, and this life is found in Jesus Christ.

THE MESSENGERS

Malachi the prophet tells us about two messengers who were to come (Malachi 3:1). They would be John the Baptist—the forerunner, and Jesus Christ the Divine messenger. Jesus brought the message of God's love for all people (John 3:16).

It was three hundred and ninety seven years before Christ came that God allowed Malachi to prophesy this message. "See I [God] will send my messenger [John the Baptist], who will prepare the way before me [Christ]. Then suddenly the Lord [Christ] you are seeking will come to his temple; the messenger of the covenant, whom you desire, will come, says the Lord Almighty" (Malachi 3:1). I'm sure you may be also wondering why the Jews didn't see this passage of Scripture as it was read from the Scrolls in their Synagogue. You may also ask yourself—why don't people hear the message of Christ, today?

JOHN THE BAPTIST AND JESUS PREACHED REPENTANCE

Some time before Christ began His earthly ministry, John the Baptist preached in the desert of Judea saying, "... Repent, for the kingdom of heaven is near" (Matthew 3:1,2). After Jesus began His ministry, He said, "I tell you, No! But unless you repent, you too will

89

all perish" (Luke 13:3).

Jesus paid a tribute to John the Baptist when He said, "This is the one about whom it is written" (Matthew 11:10). (See also Isaiah 40:3.)

WHAT IS REPENTANCE?

It is a resolve or determination to want to correct immoral behavior and lifestyle. It is a personal decision to want change. It is a promise to back away from a sinful lifestyle. It is a personal commitment, made before God, to live apart from anything that is sin. Again, we must remember, repentance is not an act or process by which we make ourselves perfect before God. It is only the changing of our minds toward sinful living. The process and hope of living a Christ-like life takes place after we are converted to Christianity through the presence and power of the Holy Spirit. This is why the Holy Spirit is called our Comforter and Helper. We make up our mind, and He then helps us to live a life which is pleasing to God. "And God is able to make all grace abound to you, so that in all things at all times, having all that you need, you will abound in every good work" (2 Corinthians 9:8). Jesus said, "... Apart from me you can do nothing" (John 15:5).

BAPTISM PURPOSED BY GOD

John the Baptist was the forerunner for the Lord Jesus. When he saw Jesus coming toward him while he was baptizing men in the Jordan River, he heard Jesus ask him to baptize Him. John said, "I need to be baptized by you, and do you come to me?" Then Jesus said to him, "Let it be so now; it is proper for us to do this to fulfill all righteousness" (Matthew 3:14-15). We learn an important lesson here about water baptism. Jesus said, "It is proper for us to do this." Jesus was an example of what God requires, which is to present our body to a water baptism because it is required by God Himself. Baptism as given by John the Baptist, was a baptism of repentance. He told those who were with him, "I baptize you with water, but he [Jesus] will baptize you with the Holy Spirit" (Mark 1:8). It was after the apostle Peter received the Holy Spirit at Pentecost that he set out to reconcile people to Christ. When Peter began to baptize people in the name of

Jesus Christ, they also *received the gift* of the Holy Spirit. Peter said, "Repent and be baptized, every one of you, in the name of Jesus Christ for the forgiveness of your sins, And you will *receive the gift* of the Holy Spirit" (Acts 2:38).

GENTILES HEAR THE GOSPEL, RECEIVE THE HOLY SPIRIT AND THEN ARE BAPTIZED

It was after Peter had preached the salvation message to the Jews that he set out to preach to the Gentiles. While he was preaching of Jesus Christ to the Gentiles, the Holy Spirit came into the hearts of those who heard the Gospel message. Acts 10:44-48 gives a chronological order of events which took place.

(1) Acts 10:44 - The Holy Spirit came down on all those who were listening.

(2) Acts 10:45 - The Jews who came with Peter were amazed that God had poured out His Holy Spirit on the Gentiles.

(3) Acts 10:46 - The Gentiles were speaking in strange tongues, praising God's greatness. (Evidence of the Spirit's presence.)

(4) Acts 10:47 - Then Peter said, "... Can anyone keep these? people from being baptized with water? They have just received the Holy Spirit just as we have."

(5) Acts 10:48 - Peter commanded them to be baptized.

It is Jesus who sends the Holy Spirit, just as He promised prior to His ascension (John 16:7). Anyone who repents and is baptized into Jesus Christ for the remission of their sins will, by God's promise, receive the gift of the Holy Spirit.

THE BEGINNING OF BAPTISM BY WATER

It first began with John the Baptist as he began to prepare the way for the coming of Christ. His baptism was a baptism of repentance. There are two applications: physical and spiritual. The physical involves sprinkling, pouring, and immersing. John the Baptist immersed Jesus in water. The Greek word for baptism in the New

Testament means "to immerse" or "dip." We will address immersion since it is the only means of baptism recorded in the Holy Bible. Water baptism is an outward testimony of an inner belief in Christ.

UNDERSTANDING SPIRITUAL IMMERSION INTO CHRIST

The spiritual aspect of being baptized into Christ [not a water baptism] may be summed up this way. When the Holy Spirit and the believer become one, then Christ lives in the believer. To the believers in Galatia, Paul said, "For all of you who have been baptized into Christ have clothed yourselves with Christ" (Galatians 3:27). To be clothed with Christ means you've been given Christ's power through the indwelling Holy Spirit. Only then can Christians trust, follow, and obey Him.

Paul explained it to the believers at Corinth this way. He said, "Don't you know that you yourselves are God's temple and that God's Spirit lives in you?" (1 Corinthians 3:16). Again, when the Spirit lives in you, so does Jesus, because they are one in the same Godhead.

A personal faith in Christ and a true conversion experience precedes receiving the gift of the Holy Spirit. After we receive the gift of the Holy Spirit, then we are able to live in Christ.

Anyone who believes Jesus Christ was raised from the dead has been given the gift of the Holy Spirit. Paul said, "... If anyone does not have the Spirit of Christ, he does not belong to Christ" (Romans 8:9).

BAPTISM AND ITS SIGNIFICANCE

Water baptism of itself does not save a soul. It is a witness and an act of obedience to what God demands. Jesus told the thief on the cross next to Jesus, that he would be in paradise with Jesus yet that same day. Obviously, he was not baptized in water (Luke 23:43). Even though this was an isolated situation, water baptism is very important according to what Jesus said to John the Baptist, "it is proper for us to do this to fulfill all righteousness" (Matthew 3:15). About water baptism, "And this water symbolizes baptism that now saves you also—not the removal of dirt from the body but the pledge of a good conscience toward God" (1 Peter 3:21). When baptism takes place, it is always in water, it is always in His death, and it is always in His resurrection (Romans 6:3,4, John 3:5, Acts 8:38).

The Bible makes no mention of infant baptism. Only the baptism of adults is noted. Many churches and assemblies of believers today who practice adult baptism still dedicate infants and small children to God until they reach baptism age. Water baptism is evidence of one's faith in the risen Lord. *When we do submit ourselves to a water baptism we make known to others our belief in what Jesus Christ has accomplished through His suffering, His death, His burial, and His resurrection.* Water baptism usually takes place before an Assembly of God's people because it is an attestation of one's belief in the purpose of Christ's death and His resurrection.

Baptism by immersion was given to all that John the Baptist baptized, including Jesus Christ. Philip asked the eunuch if he believed that Jesus Christ was the Son of God. Affirming that he did, he was baptized in the water. There is no accounting of baptism by any other form in the authorized scriptures.

The spiritual significance of baptism is recorded in Romans 6:3. Paul, speaking to believers, said, "Or don't you know that all of us who were baptized into Christ Jesus were baptized into His death." This means we who believe in Christ know with certainty that He died in our place. We know that we should have been put to death for our sins, but God knew we could do nothing for ourselves. That is why He sent His only Son to die in our place.

Water baptism is a way of identifying with Christ's death and resurrection. Because God requires water baptism, we should continue in this observance to honor God's will.

EMPHASIS UPON BELIEVING

We should always place great credence upon the Words of Christ when He said, "Whoever *believes* and is baptized will be saved, but whoever does not believe will be condemned" (Mark 16:16). It is evident that believing precedes a water baptism. The emphasis in this passage, though, is on "believing." It is not the water of baptism that saves, but it is God's grace through Jesus Christ that saves.

OTHER BIBLE PASSAGES ABOUT BAPTISM

Jesus was baptized by John the Baptist (Mark 1:10).

The Holy Spirit came upon Jesus when He came up and out of the water (Luke 3:22).

When Jesus came up out of the water, God said, "You are my Son, whom I love; with you I am well pleased" (Luke 3:22).

John the Baptist said, "I baptize you with water for repentance. But after me will come one who is more powerful than I, whose sandals I am not fit to carry. He will baptize you with the Holy Spirit and with fire" (Matthew 3:11).

Peter refers to Noah's family who were saved by water, a symbol of baptism (1 Peter 3:20-21).

Peter speaks of both repentance and baptism for the remission of sin (Acts 2:38).

"Having been buried with him in baptism and raised with him through your faith in the power of God, who raised him from the dead" (Colossians 2:12).

THE GREAT COMMISSION AND BAPTISM

"Then Jesus came to them and said, All authority in heaven and on earth has been given to me. Therefore go and make disciples of all nations, baptizing them in the name of the Father and of the Son and of the Holy Spirit" (Matthew 28:18,19).

As we read and meditate upon this passage, known as the Great Commission, two things stand out. *First,* Christ's identity with the reality of the Holy Trinity of God. *Secondly*, His words were concerning baptizing converts. Jesus has given His authority and full power of attorney to carry on the work which He started. This power of attorney is for every believer and follower of Jesus Christ. "All this is from God, who reconciled us to himself through Christ and gave us the ministry of reconciliation" (2 Corinthians 5:18).

Christ's words "baptizing them in the name of..." imparts power to help bring in the Holy Spirit. Jesus said, "And in that day you will no longer ask me anything. I tell you the truth, my Father will give you whatever you ask in my name" (John 16:23). In my name is Christ's authority to all believers to ask for and act upon those things which God calls Christians to do. Jesus wants His believers and followers to tell everyone that God will put His Spirit into them, and accept them as members into His family. When doing this, the believer fulfills his responsibility in the ministry of reconciliation.

THE THREE FOLD WITNESS

"For there are three that testify: the Spirit, the water and the blood; and the three are in agreement" (1 John 5:7,8).

Jesus was baptized in water, and so is the believer. Jesus was filled with the Holy Spirit, and so is the believer. Jesus shed His blood, and the believer is redeemed by His shed blood. It is written, we have redemption through His blood, the forgiveness of sins, according to the riches of His grace (Ephesians 1:7). Also written for our notice is how we are saved. Ephesians 2:8-9 records, **"For it is by grace you have been saved, through faith—and this not from yourselves, it is the gift of God—not by works, so that no one can boast."**

Regardless of anything, new converts should remember that their water baptism is a result of their personal faith in Christ's death and resurrection.

BAPTIZED INTO ONE SPIRIT

"For we were baptized by one Spirit into one body—whether Jews or Greeks, slave or free—and we were all given the one Spirit to drink" (1 Corinthians 12:13). This refers to a miracle whereby believers are baptized into the body of Christ. The words "baptized by one Spirit" refer to a holy occurrence, or time when a person is transformed spiritually into Christ. The same Spirit who came into Christ at His baptism does it. This is the miracle of a new birth.

"Given the one Spirit to drink" means it is the same Holy Spirit who comes into the hearts of all believers. The Apostle Paul said, "...

And if anyone does not have the Spirit of Christ, he does not belong to Christ" (Romans 8:9). The "baptized into Christ" refers to those who truly believe they belong to Christ. It is the Spirit himself who makes this possible, as we see in this next passage. "The Spirit Himself testifies with our spirit that we are God's children" (Romans 8:16). Water baptism is not an initiation rite intended to confirm someone into the Church. It is the external evidence and testimony of a most serious and sincere personal belief in Christ, and is done to fulfill God's own righteousness.

JESUS' INSTRUCTIONS TO OBEY THE COMMANDMENTS

A rich young ruler asked Jesus how he could have eternal life. Jesus, responding to the man who called Him good, said; "There is only One who is good. If you want to enter life [eternal life], obey the commandments."

The rich man asked Jesus, "Which commandments?" Jesus referred to murder, adultery, stealing, accusing others falsely, honoring of mother, father, and brotherly love. He further told him how to be perfect. He said, "Sell all you own and give it to the poor and come and follow me." The rich man who had many possessions went away in sorrow. (Read the account in Matthew 19:16-26.)

Too many people today are not willing to give up their positions and possessions which can interfere with a true commitment to God's laws. The lesson we should learn from the parable of the rich young ruler is that unless we put Christ above our positions and possessions, our commitment is weak and untrue. True Christian living demands a fighting off of the old ways of life. Christian living requires giving up all things that keep us from Christ. The lesson we learn from the parable about the rich man does have a direct relationship with repentance. How? If repentance means to turn away from anything that separates us from God, then we must consider all things that detach us from Him. If our position and possessions keep us from what He asks of us, then we must be willing to change.

Possessions possess. If we are not careful, we can easily fall into the trap of allowing our possessions to dominate our behavior. How? Through selfishness, greed, and being contemptuously proud.

Possessions are not limited only to money or the power which it represents, but also to our station in life. This was the problem with the rich young ruler who left the scene, in sorrow. He knew that Jesus was right, but he did not want to part from his earthly status. He did not want to enter a spiritual life, because he did not want to part from those things that dominated his life. Man cannot love God and continue to love the things, which keeps him from being faithful to God.

CHOICES—LOVE THE WORLD, OR CHOOSE CHRIST

Today, when man is asked to forsake the sinful pleasures of life and lifestyle, which satisfies his five senses, he usually expresses an immediate disinterest in salvation, because it requires giving up too much. He will disclaim the Holy Scriptures and call everything religious nonsense. Some professing Christians may also fall into this category. It happened in the bible account of the rich man who did not want to listen to the man [Jesus] whom he addressed as "Teacher." He walked away sad when he realized the conditions called for giving up everything to follow Christ. How about you? Are you caught in this same kind of dilemma? Where salvation is a gift in itself, the conditions set forth by God remain. "For the sinful nature desires what is contrary to the Spirit, and the Spirit what is contrary to the sinful nature. They are in conflict with each other, so that you do what you want. But, if you are led by the Spirit you are not under law [compelling force of Satan]" (Galatians 5:17- 18).

The apostle John gives us important directions. "Do not love the world or anything in the world. If anyone loves the world, the love of the Father is not in him. For everything in the world—the cravings of sinful man, the lust of his eyes and the boasting of what he has and does—comes not from the Father but from the world. The world and its desires pass away, but the man who does the will of God lives forever" (1 John 2:15-17). You may not be thinking about how long you will live, however, be assured—life passes us by quickly.

TURNING AWAY FROM OLD HABITS

Are we a product of our environment? I think it is relative. Though we are always changing, we should consider changes that will improve our standing before God, then we know we are doing right. Patterns of behavior are connected to our past. When we follow biblical principles we know that things will work out a lot smoother for us. God's principles do not change. He hates sin and demands righteousness.

IN RETROSPECT

God's will, His insight and direction are clearly understandable and remain the same. We learned what it means to repent and the need to be baptized into Christ. We learned of the prophecy and reviewed the need for believing. We read how the "Great Commission" calls for believers to go and make disciples everywhere, and how believers are gathered together in One Spirit. We read about the necessity of obeying God's commandments. With all of this hindsight, perhaps its time to make a final assessment of your own personal goals.

If you are a believer and follower of Christ, then perhaps it is easier for you. If, however, you have not had the experience of a conversion and have not yet been redeemed by the blood of Christ, then I urge you to make your peace with God through Jesus Christ. It all starts with a desire to have God's forgiveness and promise of life eternal. Yes, Jesus died on the cross for your sins too. Why not ask Christ into your life right now? God's promise that you will receive the gift of the Holy Spirit and the promise of life eternal is true.

The church does not give salvation. *Your salvation is in your hands.* Yes, it is the duty and privilege of the church to bring its people to Bible knowledge concerning the gospel of Jesus Christ. You are saved by the grace of God when you repent and believe in the resurrection of Jesus Christ. Some may think this does not apply to them because they don't murder, rape, steal, commit adultery, or commit other barbaric acts. Romans 3:23 tells us, "For all have sinned and fall short of the glory of God." *All sin leads to death. With God, sin is sin.* God makes no deals for larger or smaller sins. Unless we come to God through Christ with a solid commitment to Him, our chance of a rebirth is slim. Salvation is a gift of God (Ephesians 2:8) but the gift cannot be given until God's conditions are met. God has given man His plan of salvation. According to the Scriptures this plan includes an order of events which when followed by the seeker will satisfy our God in Heaven.

TOO MANY HAVE THE WRONG INFORMATION

If you are one of many who think going to church regularly, or supporting a church financially, or working on church committees, or being good, or praying aplenty, or just plain depending upon the church which you attend to automatically get you to heaven, then you have not been informed correctly. God's plan for man's salvation is simple. It is so simple that man still does not want to believe. Millions are misled and think they can have God apart from Jesus Christ (2 John vs 9).

Do not be fooled by doctrines that are contrary to the Holy Scriptures. It is not through precedent, or any ritual law of any order or system that salvation is found. Books written by man, including this one, is not the same as the Holy Inspired Word of God. New life begins with a true repentance and commitment to trust, follow, and obey Christ through His Holy Words.

DIVINE CALLING

"Those whom I love I rebuke and discipline. So, be earnest, and repent. Here I am! I stand at the door and knock. If anyone hears my voice and opens the door, I will come in and eat with him and he with me. To him who overcomes, I will give the right to sit with me on my throne, just as I overcame and sat down with my Father on his throne. He who has an ear, let him hear what the Spirit says to the churches" (Revelation 3:19- 22). This gracious invitation given to everyone, by Jesus Christ Himself could save your life.

"If you can? Said Jesus, everything is possible for him who believes" (Mark 9:23).

CHAPTER 9

THE NEW BIRTH

Birth is defined as the beginning of existence or the fact of being born. When we think of birth, we think of a beginning. To Nicodemus, who was a teacher of the law, Jesus declared, "I tell you the truth, no one can see the kingdom of God unless he is born again" (John 3:3). To be born means to be brought into life. We are first brought into a physical life, and then we must be brought into a spiritual life—if we want to be with God. Why? Because God is Spirit, and if we are to be with Him in eternity, we must be born of the Spirit. We are made one with Him through His own Spirit. Sin separates us from God until such time that we are made right with God.

To Nicodemus, Jesus used the words "born again" (John 3:3). Did he understand what Jesus meant by this? As a teacher, he probably understood spiritual restoration from the Old Testament (Ezekiel 36:24-27). Today we have an added advantage. The New Testament discloses everything concerning regeneration which means spiritual change, rebirth, or born again.

WHY MUST THERE BE A NEW BIRTH?

Let's reason the answer according to Scripture.

(1) *God made us for Himself* "Let us make man in our image, in our likeness..." (Genesis 1:26).

(2) *His greatest commandment is to—* "Love the Lord your God with all your heart and with all your soul and with all your mind. This is the first and greatest commandment" (Matthew 22:37,38, see also, Deuteronomy 6:5).

(3) *We cannot love God* while we are in sin, because we are separated from God through Adam's sin. "For since death [separation] came through a man..." (1 Corinthians 15:21).

(4) *Unless we are reconciled with God* through a new birth, we remain separated from Him. "All this is from God,

who reconciled us to himself through Christ..."
(2 Corinthians 5:18).

(5) *God provided a means* to everyone who believes that
Jesus Christ is the Christ "Everyone who believes that
Jesus Christ is the Christ is born of God..." (1 John 5:1).

Believing in Christ's atoning death brings with it a restoration of kinship. *Belief without proof, which is faith, is essential to a spiritual renewal.* Yes, even faith like that of a child. As Jesus said, "I tell you the truth, anyone who will not receive the kingdom of God like a little child will never enter it" (Mark 10:15).

Being born of human parents makes us human, and being born the second time, we are born of the Spirit. We would not have had our physical birth if it were not for the miracle of life itself (Psalms 139:13-16). The miracle of a new life in our second birth results in a life which is eternal. Ultimately, all who overcome will be in paradise with God forever. Do you remember what Jesus said to the thief on the cross? He said, "I tell you the truth, today you will be with me in paradise" (Luke 23:43).

New Testament Scriptures tell us that Jesus has given us a spiritual resurrection. Before conversion we are dead in our sins (Ephesians 2:2). After a commitment is made to Christ, a conversion takes place. Through faith in Christ's resurrection, anyone can have a spiritual resurrection, which means to be raised from a dead position before God.

Sin brings with it death: "Then, after desire has conceived, it gives birth to sin; and sin, when it is full grown, gives birth to death [meaning separation from God]" (James 1:15). God wants man to be restored, so that once again God can enjoy what He has created. This requires a new birth which is spiritual. We are born of the Spirit, when we come to Christ.

JESUS MAKES KNOWN THE NEED FOR A NEW BIRTH

In view of what Jesus said in John 3:3, "... Unless he is born again..." let us concentrate on the word *again* which means *once more.* Born from the womb of our mother is a physical birth. Born by the

Spirit of God is spiritual birth. The word "born," being descriptive tells us that something has happened, and the word "again" means something else happens.

It is through believing in Christ's bodily resurrection from the grave that we, through God's mercy and grace, become overcomers through our new birth. *This new birth does not mean we just turned over a new leaf in our old lives. It means we have begun a new life, and this new life rests in the power that God gives. This power comes from the Holy Spirit.* Because Jesus Christ and the Holy Spirit are one, we then become one with them. When this happens, life then is not the same. That is why God's Word says, "... The old has gone, the new has come" (2 Corinthians 5:17). This passage is full of great distinctions in the new believer's life. Through God's grace, he is a new being; his old ways are dead. Because new things have taken over, a new spiritual life is formed. We are made right with God because of Christ. The new follower of Christ is now able to grow spiritually according to God's ways, and is made complete by God's power. Jesus said to Nicodemus, "... No one can enter the kingdom of God unless he is born of water and of the Spirit" (John 3:5). "Of water and of the Spirit" may be explained this way. (1) Physical birth requires water, conversely, spiritual birth requires Spirit. (2) At the specific moment of conversion, sins are washed away and a regeneration or spiritual change through the Holy Spirit, takes effect, through God's grace.

NEW BIRTH MAKES US A MEMBER OF CHRIST'S BODY

This chapter is about a new birth. The word "new" is intended to add something to what has already happened. New birth implies change. This change is real because it is new. Until a man or woman is reborn in the sight of God, there is no hope toward total forgiveness for sins, nor the hope of living with God forever. Sin must be removed before we can be with Him in earth or heaven and this is accomplished only through a new birth. Jesus is the only means that God has provided for anyone to become a member of Christ's Body, the Church. There is a difference between role membership in a church, and being a baptized member in Christ's Spiritual Body. *The Church is the collective body of believers who strive to live repentant lives.*

Jesus' prayer for all future believers in John 17:20 says, "I pray also for those who will believe in me through their message." Their message refers to the change in the believer's life and what he does with that change. A change in attitude, lifestyle, and behavior should be reflected in our Christian walk and testimony for Christ.

NEW BIRTH MEANS REGENERATION
OR SPIRITUAL CHANGE

Regeneration means there is a spiritual change. This change is made possible only through an act of God. The result of regeneration is to have one's moral fabric changed. It is a change from an unrighteous state of sinfulness to a position of righteousness with God. Why and how? Because God keeps Satan's hands tied (1 John 5:18). It is only with God's help that the Christian can have spiritual victory and maturity. How does this spiritual change occur? "He saved us, not because of righteous things we had done, but because of His mercy. He saved us through the washing of rebirth and renewal by the Holy Spirit, whom he poured out on us generously through Jesus Christ our Savior" (Titus 3:5).

One might assume that everyone who attends a Christian church has been born again. Not so. Many people in Christian churches today do not understand a new birth, or regeneration. Why? Because it may not have been preached, or it may not have been heard. Many preachers preach to soothe—listening ears. When their job is on the line, they stay away from things that upset people. The other reason may be that too many people are more faithful to their religion which does not save a soul. Too much religion and pride was the problem with the Pharisees. The truth is, without being born again; there is no new birth. A true believer is one who has been born again or born from above. The early church at Antioch was filled with a mixture of Jews and Gentiles. Their common goal was to learn to follow the teachings of Christ. It was here in Antioch that the disciples were first called Christians (Acts 11:26).

PARABLE OF TWO BUILDERS
AND WHY WE NEED GOD'S PLAN

According to Jesus Himself, not all who claim to be Christians will be allowed into their long awaited heavenly home. Here is what He said: "Why do you call me, Lord, Lord, and do not do what I say? I will show you what he is like who comes to me, hears my words, and puts them into practice. He is like a man building a house, who dug down deep and laid the foundation on the rock [a wise builder]. When a flood came, the torrent struck that house but could not shake it, because it was well built. But the one who hears my words and does not put them into practice is like a man who built a house on the ground without a foundation [an unwise builder]. The moment the torrent struck that house, it collapsed and its destruction was complete" (Luke 6:46-49). Is your spiritual foundation built upon the Word of God, or upon the words of men?

BORN AGAIN... FROM IMPERFECTION TO PERFECTION

God wants us for Himself and He makes possible our spiritual conversion—from imperfection to perfection. Perfection by His standards. No one can add even one thing to Christ's atoning work at the cross. "For we are God's workmanship, created in Christ Jesus to do good works, which God prepared in advance for us to do" (Ephesians 2:10).

Before conversion, we are in sin. After conversion, we are without sin before God. Why? Because our sins were paid for at the cross. Because we were in sin, we were imperfect in God's eyes. We become perfect before God the moment we are spiritually reborn, not because of what we do, but of what Christ did at the cross.

What do we do about the sins we might commit after we have given ourselves to Christ? God covers us here also. "... But if anybody does sin, we have one who speaks to the Father in our defense—Jesus Christ, the Righteous One" (1 John 2:1).

When we are reborn, sin no longer has dominion over the believer. *This is the victory and the miracle of the Cross for all who will believe.* Two things take place the moment we are converted: our sins are forgiven and the Holy Spirit comes into us. At this moment, we are joined together with God spiritually, and forever. Believers have been given the power to overcome sin through the Spirit's presence (Romans 8:13).

People are not always sensitive to their sinfulness. Some may even feel they are good and don't sin. The Bible says, "If we claim to be without sin, we deceive ourselves, and the truth is not in us" (1 John 1:8). There are those whose sins are very grave. Deep down in their hearts they know their sins but do not know what to do about them. They may want to get away from their deep sinning but are skeptical in asking for God's help. Through a new birth, all this will change. We can know with certainty that through Christ all things are possible. There is only one way for man to cut out his old sinfulness—through the blood of Christ. It is through Him that we are regenerated or morally reformed.

EACH NEW BIRTH BRINGS JOY TO GOD'S ANGELS

We often admire or appreciate a newborn cat, rabbit, deer, dog, or any animal of our liking. To the eyes of a normal mother toward her newborn baby, words cannot describe her feelings of ecstasy. To God and the angels in heaven, the rebirth of any person brings great joy. "In the same way, I tell you, there is rejoicing in the presence of the angels of God over one sinner who repents" (Luke 15:10).

Here again, joy is expressed in the Word of God when a sinner repents. "I tell you that in the same way there will be more rejoicing in heaven over one sinner who repents than over ninety-nine righteous persons who do not need to repent" (Luke 15:7).

A new birth is a joy, be it in earth or in heaven. Life is very precious. Ask a man who is told he is going to die. He will do anything to save his physical life. He will deplete his assets and go through many deep struggles and pain to hold onto life. In many cases, man cannot hold on to his physical life and he loses it. When the physical life is gone, it's gone. Spiritual life has a different hope, and that hope is in a new birth and a new life.

DOES MAN HAVE TO CLEAN HIMSELF UP
AND THEN COME TO JESUS?

Absolutely not! If that were the case, no one could have a new birth; no one could become saved. With a repentant heart, we come to Christ as we are, and He does the cleaning up. Important to remember is that Christ's shed blood and His death have already paid for your sins and mine. The debt has been paid. We have been redeemed "with the precious blood of Christ, a lamb without blemish or defect..." (1 Peter 1:19). Christ died for all sinners. The debt He paid was His personal sacrifice. His suffering and death was for every individual who ever was and who is to come into this world.

Were you born when Jesus died for your sins? Of course not, God, who is able to see ahead and know all things before they happen, knew those who would share in the inheritance which Jesus made possible. It was in the beginning that He purposed our holy calling. Someone said, "God does not call the qualified; He qualifies the called." So, if you have not been saved by His grace, may I ask you then—what are you waiting for?

GOD'S FOREKNOWLEDGE

No one should try to argue with God. The Bible tells us in 2 Timothy 1:9 about God's foreknowledge: "Who has saved us and called us to a holy life—not because of anything we have done but because of his own purpose and grace. This grace was given us in Christ Jesus before the beginning of time." Our praise to Him must never end. Let's praise Him again and again for His deep love and compassion through His only Son.

WE LEARN TO SERVE GOD AFTER WE ARE SAVED

The true Christian is not just a member of a church. He is one who learns and follows the teachings of Christ. This requires a firm commitment. Jesus said to His disciples, "If anyone would come after me, he must deny himself and take up his cross and follow me. For whoever wants to save his life will lose it, but whoever loses his life for me will find it" (Matthew 16:24-25). The believer, upon giving his life to serve Christ, will find a good purpose for living. This kind of living means the Christian turns not inward, but outward, in serving others according to Christ's love. Serving really means to help others in the spirit of God's love. In this way, we truly become His servants.

To lose one's life means to give up all things that lead to sin. The true Christian will deny himself many things which otherwise would have remained "status quo." Many, in times past, have even lost their lives for the Master. Stephen, a martyr in the early church, was stoned to death because he criticized the Sanhedrin concerning the death of Jesus.

JESUS DEFINES TWO THINGS ABOUT FLESH AND SPIRIT

A new birth must precede a true walk with God. Until people come to Jesus Christ in truth and in faith, they fool themselves. Why? Because they are not yet spiritually reborn. Jesus said we must be born again. When the miracle of a new birth is given, so also does a new relationship and fellowship with God begin. What is man expected to do because he is flesh and not spirit? This is exactly what Jesus is telling us in John 3:6, "Flesh gives birth to flesh, but the Spirit gives birth to spirit." A new birth makes us complete, without any imperfections in God's eyes. It must not be perceived as a procedure but as a miracle.

Many people today do not feel right with God. They may have had certain emotional religious experiences or perhaps have relied upon a ritual church service only to find out that nothing has changed. If that is the case with you or anyone you know, then may I suggest you come before God in spirit and truth? God will honor anyone who will come to Him. We present ourselves through hearing and obeying the Word of God. Jesus said you must be born again.

HOW DOES ONE KNOW FOR CERTAIN
THEY HAVE HAD A NEW BIRTH?

Jesus said, "He who is not with me is against me, and he who does not gather with me scatters" (Matthew 12:30). Are you gathering together with Christ in prayer, in witnessing to others, and living through faith in His promises? Or have you scattered from Christ? Have you laid your claim to a new birth? Yes I know there are many who think that because they were baptized as a baby or a young child, they belong to Jesus. But, that's not what the Scriptures say. There is no middle road, no maybe, no perhaps. It is one way or the other. Many people know the story of Christ's life and purpose, and still may not have had their new birth. I could say, I know my country is the

Land of opportunity, and waiting for me are great treasures, but unless I do something about that opportunity, nothing will happen. We can look at salvation in a similar manner. For anyone to receive the inheritance which God has prepared for them, they must personally do something about it.

To become born again, we must respond to God's call. Salvation is not automatic. Our physical birth was by the will of man. In contrast, our spiritual birth is not by the will of man but by the will of God (John 1:12,13). Many people attend church regularly and may be great givers of their time and talents. They may have great compassion for the poor and the hungry but may not know a thing about a new birth. They may have been depending upon someone else beside Christ. Unknowingly, many fall prey to unscriptural church laws, false teachings, or doctrines formulated by the minds of men.

True believers and followers of Christ know they have an inheritance, and it is only through God's Word that they know for certain. Here is a sample of this. "And you also were included in Christ when you heard the word of truth, the gospel of your salvation" (Ephesians 1:13). Have you claimed this passage? Are you consciously aware of this passage? *God has given everyone the opportunity to have their richest treasure ever, which is eternal life.* This is the single greatest inheritance we can have. Unless we reach out and take advantage of the means by which God has provided, we forfeit the gift of life.

READING AND HEARING THE WORD OF GOD

The written record of salvation in chapters 2 and 10 in the Book of Acts teaches us the significance of God's instructions. It tells us about the Jews and Gentiles and what happened to them; they heard the Word preached, received the Holy Spirit, and were baptized. God's Word embodies truth concerning the distinct happenings to those who were among the first to be saved through the Gospel message. It is wise to read and believe what has been written for our use and application. *Hearing the Word of God, repenting, and confessing Jesus Christ through our faith is to have a new birth.*

THE BELIEVER'S GUARANTEE FROM THE HOLY SPIRIT

Salvation is the saving of a soul from the consequences if sin. Believing in the Gospel of Jesus Christ is necessary for anyone to have salvation. Believing is the outcome of our faith. If there is no faith, there is no salvation. The issue of faith must be addressed, and *the issue of a new birth must be dealt with before it is too late.* This next passage applies to you personally, either in a past, present, or future tense. The secret lies in hearing. "And you also were included in Christ when you heard the word of truth, the gospel of your salvation. Having believed, you were marked in him with a seal, the promised Holy Spirit, who is a deposit guaranteeing our inheritance until the redemption of those who are God's possession—to the praise of his glory" (Ephesians 1:13,14).

The worldly man counts his money, takes stern action toward his possessions when required, and, above all, he would give anything to live longer. For a variety of reasons, he lacks the earnestness and interest in his real and true godly inheritance. How about you? Have you laid claim to the inheritance which God has for you? Are you certain of this second birth which Jesus talks about? All saved people will quickly attest their standing before God. Listen to these next words of Christ as He says, "For everyone born of God overcomes the world. This is the victory that overcomes the world, even our faith" (1 John 5:4).

Some people do not take the time to understand what it means to be born again, yet they will trust their life insurance policies until the day they die and not be around to collect the benefits.

Compare this with the God of all creation who sent His Son to die for the sins of mankind. "In him we have redemption..." (Ephesians 1:7). This redemption is not like the redemption of our insurance policies because they can change, but God guarantees His policy. "... the Holy Spirit of God, with whom you were sealed for the day of redemption" (Ephesians 4:30).

An individual should know whether a new birth has taken place. There are some who may not be knowledgeable about the Bible's call for a new birth, or being born again, but now you know. Yes, some today, because of their religious experiences, have accepted a non-scriptural doctrine and may not know any more than Nicodemus knew about the necessity of being born again.

THE POWER AND MERCY OF GOD

"In the past God spoke to our forefathers through the prophets at many times and in various ways, but in these last days he has spoken to us by His Son, whom he appointed heir of all things, and through whom he made the universe. The Son is the radiance of God's glory and the exact representation of his being, sustaining all things by his powerful word. After he had provided purification for sins, he sat down at the right hand of the Majesty in heaven" (Hebrews 1:1-3). Are you quite sure of your second birthday? If not, then don't delay another minute. God does everything in love. He adds to our life here on earth. He adds to us His Holy Spirit, who gives us the ability to understand the Bible and live in peace (1 John 2:27, Acts 2:38).

THE BELIEVER'S ASSURANCE OF LIFE ETERNAL

He gives the believer this promise: "I give them eternal life, and they shall never perish; no one can snatch them out of my hand" (John 10:28).

According to the written Word of God, *He will not abandon the person who really and truly has had his second birth and has placed his trust in Him.* The desire to sin leaves the saved person, and a new nature takes over. This new nature allows the believer to come to God in a deeper way. Certainly not according to any of man's religious systems, but through the Blood of Christ. God is now on our side, His Spirit lives in us, and we have a whole new agenda to follow and believe. The believer will come to know with certainty that he is the receiver of a great inheritance. This inheritance is what God's plan of salvation is all about. He's waiting patiently for all people to acknowledge His Son. If you have this heavenly gift, then why not find someone who does not, and help them to come to know the love of God? *"If you can? said Jesus, everything is possible for him who believes" (Mark 9:23).*

CHAPTER 10

THE ABUNDANT LIFE

Who doesn't want an abundant life? The average American is caught up in the dream of having one of everything. To have everything in abundance is the fantasy of many today. Lotto players across the country feverishly hope to win—against odds which are staggering to the imagination of the conservative mind. Some people want so much to have things in abundance that they spend themselves into a non-recovery debt. Many are obsessed with desire for abundance of material things which, in the end, clutter up the closets of America. In vogue today is a hunger to have all sort of material things: property, cars, clothes, second homes, boats, airplanes, and the list goes on and on. People can't seem to get enough money and are busier than ever keeping up with sports, recreation, and vacations. The mood for years has been more of everything, and that never turns out to be enough.

This chapter is not intended to talk about the matters of the abundance of material or financial possessions, although they do make a negative impact upon the real subject of this chapter. There are other things that are more important. We will address those things.

REAL AND TRUE SECURITY

Security means different things to different people. Real and true security in a spiritual realm has no relationship with material or financial things. Freedom from insecure things like doubt, anxiety, or fear is a concern to us all. The greater concern should be, what will happen if we die before we make our peace with God? Being grounded in honest and true principles wins many friends, but does not bring spiritual security. Real and true security is realized only when Jesus Christ has first place in our hearts. *Where many want to believe God's promises are sure, they are not willing to deepen their commitment to God to be sure.* It is only when trouble arises that we reach for God. Unless we make the right choice before its too late, the right choice may never be made. Unless we accept God's plan for spiritual restoration, we have no real and true security. Those who lean upon Jesus Christ for their eternal security will never be abandoned by God (John 10:28).

Man may think he has it all—money, position, and fame—only to find out in the closing days of his life he can't take any of these things with him. Man usually finds out too late that he chose the wrong path in life.

God told Adam, "Cursed is the ground because of you; through painful toil you will eat of it all the days of your life" (Genesis 3:17). Therefore, hope becomes real when we think about God's new covenant through His Son. "And this is what he promised us—even eternal life" (1 John 2:25). You will be interested to know how God feels about His promises. He said, "The Lord is not slow in keeping His promise, as some understand slowness. He is patient with you, not wanting anyone to perish, but everyone to come to repentance" (2 Peter 3:9).

GOD WILL TAKE CARE OF YOUR NEEDS

God knows all of our needs and greater things are yet to come. He supplies seed for the sower and bread to the eater. *We must remember His law of proportionate reward. To whom much is given, much is expected.* I know people who always seem to give away more than they have and somehow God restores their needs. It is not only material giving which God believes is important, but all other ways too. Giving our time, talent, understanding, compassion, counseling, and loaning money in time of dire need are some of the many ways we can fulfill God's law of proportionate reward. Read 2 Corinthians 9:6-9 and Luke 12:48. Abundant life or having life to its fullest includes security and refuge.

ABUNDANT GRACE

Paul's first letter to Timothy reflects a spirit of thankfulness to Jesus Christ for strength in his work. Paul thanked God for electing him into service, because he remembers how he spoke evil of God, persecuted, and insulted Him. He was especially thankful for God's mercy and abundant grace that was poured out on him (1 Timothy 1:12-14).

Paul was satisfied being under God's grace even when he was suffering. He begged God to take away his suffering, which God did not do. He knew he was under God's grace of undeserved and unmerited mercy. Anyone who has given their life to Christ receives a distinction that cannot be found in any other way. *This distinction is in the sufficiency of His Grace.* Even under hardship, the immovable thorn in Paul's flesh caused him to reflect on what the Lord said; "My grace is sufficient for you, for my power is made perfect in weakness." Therefore I [Paul] will boast the more gladly about my weakness, so that Christ's power may rest on me." Read the account in 2 Corinthians 12: 1-10.

ABUNDANT PROVISIONS
God provides those who belong to Him the fruit of righteousness. The fruit of righteousness is peace and joy. We should always keep in mind that material possessions pass away, but what we learn about spirit things will stay with us. Paul encourages us to maintain a posture of sincerity in our Christian walk so that we will be blameless until Christ comes.

AN ABUNDANT ENTRANCE
The Bible tells us in 2 Peter 1:11, "And you will receive a rich welcome into the eternal kingdom of our Lord and Savior Jesus Christ." These full rights in God's kingdom will be liberal and abundant compared to our earthly status. Until we become believers, there is no hope of coming to God's kingdom and having an abundant life. Scripture tells us that eternal security rests in Jesus Christ. He is the only way to God.

ABUNDANT POWER
The Christian has great hope in these New Testament times because the Holy Spirit keeps the Christian in his faith. If you say you are a Christian then you know you are not controlled by a sinful nature, but by the Holy Spirit, if the Spirit of God lives in you. If the Spirit of Christ is not in you, you do not belong to Christ (Romans 8:9). Because the Holy Spirit lives in the believer, he has great power

and knowledge, because the Holy Spirit is the teacher of truth. It is a frightening thing to come to know that you are apart from God. Most everyone has given some thought to what will happen when they die. If you want to know with certainty that you will be with God forever, then come to know the great secret of life, which is given freely, and abundantly to those who sincerely want Christ to be in their lives. Unfortunately, many people never go far enough. They are either too busy to find out, or they think religion is just religion, with little or no true value.

ABUNDANT LIFE AND PARADISE

In Revelation 2:7, Jesus says, "He who has an ear, let him hear what the Spirit says to the churches. To him who overcomes, I will give the right to eat from the tree of life, which is in the paradise of God."

What is this paradise? Paradise is mentioned only three times in the Bible. Paul tells of a man who was caught up in paradise. He said, "I know a man in Christ who fourteen years ago was caught up to the third heaven. He heard things, things that man is not permitted to tell" (2 Corinthians 12: 2-4). Jesus told the thief on the cross that he would be with Him in paradise that same day.

Paradise is not described in any way that could give us a hint to what it is like. However, we can be sure it will be like something we have never seen before. Jesus said, "In my Father's house are many rooms; if it were not so, I would have told you, I will come back and take you to be with me that you also may be where I am. You know the way to the place where I am going" John 14:3-4). The word "house" in Greek is "Oikia," it means dwelling place. To be with Jesus in His dwelling place requires no advance notice or description to satisfy this writer. The very idea of being with God, His Son, and His Holy Spirit is all I need to know. If we follow what Jesus said about listening to Him and overcoming all barriers, we should expect to be with Him in paradise.

SPIRITUAL PROGRESS

The abundant life which Jesus mentioned in John 10:10 is relative to the larger picture of life. He said, "... I have come that they may have life, and have it to the full." This life is eternal and with it, there will be many great rewards. Just knowing how much God, who created the Universe, does for us everyday is very satisfying to know. *Believing that God sent His Son Jesus to die for our sins gives the believer the keys to His abounding grace.* To possess the knowledge and hope of being with God when we leave this earth is a great source of comfort; it is having a joy that has never been known. It is a kind of peace within the soul of the man that comes no other way. When a loved one dies, the survivors are more joyful when they know the deceased was born again in the Spirit of God prior to his physical death.

TESTIMONY OF THE WORD ITSELF

The Apostle Peter taught those who were scattered throughout the northern part of Asia Minor to always give thanks to God for His great mercy. God's mercy comes to those who believe in Christ and His resurrection. *We have New Hope and look forward to many rich blessings which God holds in heaven for all who are in obedience to, and believe in Christ.* Our assurance of this is reflected in what Peter said in 1 Peter 1:3-5. "Praise be to the God and Father of our Lord Jesus Christ! In his great mercy, he has given us new birth into a living hope through the resurrection of Jesus Christ from the dead. Also, an inheritance that can never perish, spoil or fade. It is kept in heaven for you and it is *shielded by God's power* until the coming of the salvation that is ready to be revealed in the last time." The words of Peter "shielded by God's power" are referring to the Holy Spirit's presence in the believer. Also, careful consideration should be given to those who think they are Christians and do not fully understand the condition of God's promises. It is worth repeating Romans 8:9 again which says, "You, however, are controlled not by the sinful nature but *by the Spirit*, if the Spirit of God lives in you...." How about you? Do you know that the Holy Spirit lives in you? If you know it and believe it, then you know that you are shielded by God's power. Any deviation from God's Word is dangerous.

If the many millions upon millions of people would open their eyes to the Holy Scriptures which reveal God's mercy and grace, truth would be the authority and false teaching would end. After all, deceptive religious teachings and traditions continue to cloud the glorious grace of God in many churches that claim to be Christian.

THE ABUNDANT LIFE WILL NOT TOUCH EVERYONE

Multitudes of people in this world do not believe in the Gospel of Jesus Christ. These are called the Antichrists. They are described in 1 John 2:22. "Who is the liar? It is the man who denies that Jesus is the Christ. Such a man is the antichrist—he denies the Father and the Son."

He also refers to them in 2nd John verse 7, "Many deceivers, who do not acknowledge Jesus Christ as coming in the flesh, have gone out into the world. And such person is the deceiver and the Antichrist."

John further said, in verse 9, that whoever does not stay with the teachings of Christ or acts in violation of the doctrine of Jesus Christ, does not have God. Pretty potent words, wouldn't you say so?

FALSE PROPHETS AND HOW WE KNOW THEM

Here is how we know the Spirit is of God—believing that Jesus Christ came in the flesh. Those who don't believe and confess that Jesus came in the flesh are against Christ (1 John 4:2-3). *There will be no abundant life for those who accept and live in false doctrine.* God hates deceivers and tells us to have nothing to do with them (2nd John vs 10). This does not mean we ignore them; it means we do not join their beliefs.

THE TREE OF LIFE (EVERLASTING)

The tree of life was also planted in the midst of the Garden of Eden along with the tree of knowledge, of good and evil. It was this tree of knowledge from which God forbade Adam to eat. *The tree of life represents never- ending life with God. This is the tree which Jesus promised to the believer when he said, "To him who overcomes" (Revelation 3:21).* This tree was not the forbidden tree, but it was planted along side the forbidden tree of knowledge of good and evil. God put Adam and Eve out of the Garden—including their descendants, the whole human race. Jesus' invitation to overcomers is to the tree of life, which is everlasting life, and will produce an everlasting abundant life.

TO HIM THAT OVERCOMES JESUS GIVES THESE PROMISES

(1) *LIFE ETERNAL.* To him who overcomes I will give the right to eat from the tree of life (Revelation 2:7).

(2) *NO JUDGMENT FOR SINS.* He who overcomes will not be hurt at all by the second death (Revelation 2:11).

(3) *SPIRITUAL SUSTENANCE.* To him who overcomes I will give some of the hidden manna (Revelation 2:17).

(4) *TO RULE WITH CHRIST.* To him who overcomes and does my will to the end, I will give authority over the nations (Revelations 2:26).

(5) *SET APART FOR GOD AND MADE PURE.* He who overcomes will, like them, be dressed in white. I will never blot out his name from the book of life, but will acknowledge his name before my Father and his angels (Revelation 3:5).

(6) *IMMOVABLE POSITION.* Him who overcomes I will make a pillar in the temple of my God. Never again will he leave it (Revelation 3:12).

(7) *HIGH POSITION.* To him who overcomes, I will give the right to sit with me on my throne, just as I overcame and sat down with My Father on His Throne (Revelation 3:21).

RECEIVING THE BLESSINGS GOD PROMISED

His promises are sure. The believer being made an heir with Christ will have everlasting peace with God. Jesus promises His believers and followers they will become His sons. *Testing is part of the Christian's life.* The believer's salvation is certain. Enduring to the end brings rewards beyond belief.

"He who overcomes will inherit all this, and I will be his God, and he will be My son" (Revelation 21:7).

TRIUMPH THROUGH CHRIST

Christ Jesus had the victory over Satan through His sacrifice. Christ's death was in place of the death which we deserve. It is because of Jesus and His one- time sacrifice that we have victory.

"They [believers] overcame him [Satan] by the blood of the Lamb and by their word of their testimony; they did not love their lives so much as to shrink from death" (Revelation 12:11). Faithful believers are freed from Satan's control. If they are living in the Word of God, they will speak for Christ in all situations.

Paul also talked to the Corinthians about having a spiritual victory. He said, "Do you not know that in a race all the runners run, but only one gets the prize? Run in such a way as to get the prize" (1 Corinthians 9:24). The Christian's life should not in any way be dead. We are made to serve God and His purposes.

THE LORD'S FINAL INSTRUCTIONS

"Blessed are those who wash their robes [meaning living according to God's commandments], that they may have the right to the tree of life and may go through the gates into the city [God's kingdom] (Revelation 22:14). *Obedience to the Word of God must dominate the Christian's behavior.* To resist God's Word or remain unyielding to it, is a willful behavior which will be subject to God's judgment. *Obedience is more important than rituals, sacrifices, or ceremonies.* Obedience to God's decrees are primary in our individual behavior and the church at large. Anyone who professes Christ and does not obey Christ is only fooling himself. The Christian who is truly born again is able to grow through the power of the Holy Spirit and not through his own rootstock. In honesty, we well remember how we were in our old life. The new life, given to the born again believer, is different. What has changed? God's Word gives us the answer. "His divine power has given us everything we need for life and godliness through our knowledge of him who called us by his own glory and goodness" (2 Peter 1:3).

118

The person who loves Jesus will obey His teachings. Then, God the Father and Jesus will come in and live in the believer (John 14:23). When this happens—self-control, knowledge, endurance, godliness, kindliness, and brotherly affection will take on a new meaning. These attributes then bring a kind of peace which passes our own understanding. Anyone who is truly born from above will share in the excellence of these divine attributes. The believer then will not abandon his faith in Jesus Christ and will be given full glory when he enters the Kingdom of our Lord and Savior Jesus Christ (2 Peter 1:3-11). (Other passages to read are John 3:6, 14:17 and 2 Corinthians 5:21.)

The believer and follower of Christ has so much to be thankful for. Peter said, "For you have been born again, not of perishable seed, but of imperishable seed, through the living and enduring word of God" (1 Peter 1:23). To be born again by the "Word of God" and a seed, which cannot die, means, we are children of a parent who is immortal. How great is our God in heaven.

THE CHRISTIAN WALK

The Christian's walk should be the most interesting and most exciting event ever to have taken place. Once born from above, several periods of development and growth should follow. These events or happenings should be recognized and should be most pleasing to the heart. These occurrences or happenings are the evidence of God's grace. The fact that these events have taken place or are in progress, are the experiences all followers of Christ have. A follower is one who pursues. To pursue means that you plan to overtake or to chase after. So then, "... Let us run with perseverance the race marked out for us" (Hebrews 12:1).

If you are a Christian, and discover that going to church is a not interesting and is burdensome, or that your Christian experience is not what it should be, then perhaps you should take another look. The order of events shown here should play an important part in discovering some new and interesting Biblical facts.

119

There are seven stages which the believer should have experienced in his lifetime.

Stage 1   *THE TIME OF OUR NATURAL OR PHYSICAL BIRTH.* David the Psalmist affirms this wonder. "I praise you because I am fearfully and wonderfully made; your works are wonderful, I know that full well" (Psalms 139:14).

Stage 2   *THE TIME WHEN REPENTANCE BEGINS AND CONVERSION HAS TAKEN PLACE.* This decision is the most important resolution a person can make in his or her life. It is the changing of one's mind toward sin, a change to the better, morally. Without this commitment the third stage is impossible (Matthew 4:17).

Stage 3   *THE TIME OF OUR SECOND BIRTH.* To be born again, or born of the Spirit. Jesus said, "I tell you the truth, no one can enter the kingdom of God unless he is born of water and the Spirit. Flesh gives birth to flesh, but the Spirit gives birth to spirit" (John 3:5,6)

Stage 4   *THE TIME WHEN THE GIFT OF THE HOLY SPIRIT* comes into the newly converted person (Acts 2:38). Luke reminds us what Joel the prophet said in Acts 2:17. (See Joel 2:28). "... I will pour out my Spirit on all people ..." This began at Pentecost and is still happening to all who are born again today. Receiving this gift allows all believers to enter into a personal relationship and fellowship with God. Prior to receiving the gift of the Holy Spirit, fellowship with God is not possible, because sin separates man from God.

Stage 5   ***THE TIME WHEN OBEDIENT AND FAITHFUL LIVING DOMINATE THE BELIEVER'S LIFE.*** Believers are to carefully plan their lives and through obedience follow Christ's teachings. Obedience comes from faith, and faith comes when we sincerely listen to the Word of God (Romans 1:5 and 10:17).

Stage 6   ***THE TIME WHEN TRUE WORSHIP AND SERVICE BEGIN.*** True worship is completed only in "Spirit and truth" (John 4:24). The believer, having been given the gift of the Holy Spirit (Acts 2:38), is now helped by the Holy Spirit to worship in truth and serve God. Service means to be totally committed to serving Christ.

Stage 7   ***THE TIME WHEN A TRUE CHRISTIAN WALK COMMENCES. (Christ-likeness in behavior).*** It always brings spiritual growth and it is called for by God. Here are God's instructions. " Your attitude should be the same as Christ Jesus" (Phillippians 2:5). "Therefore, prepare your minds for action; be self controlled, set your hope fully on the grace to be given you when Jesus Christ is revealed" (1 Peter 1:13). "This is to my Father's glory, that you bear much fruit, showing yourselves to be my disciples" (John 15:8).

What stage are you in?

If stage 3 has not taken place, you need to begin stage 2 which is to repent and submit to Christ.

If stages 2 and 3 have taken place, you should be in stage 4 and know it.

If stage 4 has taken place, you are in stage 5 living in faithful obedience.

If stages 4 and 5 have taken place, then you should be in stage 6 and feel the joy of worship and service.

If stages 2 through 6 have taken place, then you are truly walking with Christ and witnessing for Him. No one becomes a Christian by chance.

Christians are those who have been redeemed and know it. If you question either being redeemed or saved perhaps you should take another look. Saved means the miracle of a new spiritual life has begun. Redeemed means you were bought with the price. Only the redeemed can "... worship by the Spirit of God" (Philippians 3:3). Why? With God's Spirit having been given to the redeemed, they are able to worship in Spirit and truth, because the Spirit is in them.

Stage 6 is a time for rejoicing because God has taken over the life of the one who would otherwise be lost forever. Don't be shocked at hearing that only those who belong to God can worship him in Spirit and truth. God's Word does not lie.

Stage 7 is a time when a Christ-like behavior dominates our Christian walk.

The Christian walk means we are to be prepared for:

Tests and trials.	1 Peter 1:6,7
To live uprightly and in moderation.	Proverbs 13:6
To live with expectation to the promises of God.	1 Peter 1:3,4
To live without returning to evil desires.	1 Peter 1:14
To live blamelessly. God demands a holy living.	Ephesians 1:4
To act only on those things which honor God.	Proverbs 3:9
To love one another in a pure way.	John 15:12

THE BLESSINGS TO COME

All believers have been saved by grace. God's Word says that the Christian should live with a firm hope in the blessings which will come with Christ (1 Peter 1:3-16). We find our true identity in Christ when we walk with Him. "...To obey is better than sacrifice" (1 Samuel 15:22).

WORDS OF ENCOURAGEMENT FROM
JOHN THE APOSTLE

The Apostle John, in 1 John 4:1-6, gives the Christian uplifting and special words of counsel. We should know to whom we are to listen. Many profess Christ, but do not confess Christ as having come in the flesh. They just talk about Him and do nothing else. John is careful to tell us we should test them so that doctrine can be quickly identified.

He said, "Dear friends, do not believe every spirit, but test the spirit to see whether they are from God, because many false prophets have gone out into the world" (1 John 4:1).

CHRIST IS MAN'S LAST HOPE

Adam and Eve, through disobedience, committed the first sin. Their descendants still bear Adam's sin consequence. The coming of Christ became man's first and last hope of being forgiven and losing his sinful characteristics (1 John 5:18). The disobedience of Adam brought a curse on all, but obedience through Jesus Christ brings everlasting peace and God's promise of everlasting life.

Through believing in the Gospel of Jesus Christ, the believer becomes the recipient of forgiveness, partaker of a divine nature, eternal life, and the gift of the Holy Spirit (2 Peter 1:4 and Acts 2:38). The advent of the believer's new nature ushers in a new hope for the people of God.

Jesus said in Revelation 22:12, "Behold, I am coming soon! My reward is with me, and I will give to everyone according to what he has done."

WHAT DOES CHRIST'S RESURRECTION MEAN
TO ALL WHO BELIEVE?

Jesus told Martha, "I am the resurrection and the life. He who believes in me will live, even though he dies; and whoever lives

♦ believes in me will never die. Do you believe this?" (John 11:25,26). Jesus had talked with Martha prior to His death, and Martha said she did believe this. *The resurrection of Jesus Christ is central to the Doctrine of Christianity.* Paul, in 1 Corinthians 15:14, said, "And if Christ has not been raised, our preaching is useless and so is your faith."

He said further in vs 17, "And if Christ has not been raised, your faith is futile; you are still in your sins." From this we understand there would be no forgiveness for our sins if it were not for Christ. There would be no hope of heaven. There would be no church to go to, there would be no Christian faith, and there would be no hope of an abundant life—if it were not for Christ's resurrection.

Because Jesus was raised from the dead, we will also be raised on that last day. We will be with other believers and followers forever. Jesus visited His disciples for a very short time after His resurrection from the grave. He then returned to the Father in heaven. He will come again. This time it will be for all who have confessed Him and believe that He is the Son of the living God. Do we have something to get excited about, something to hope for? Yes, and without any doubt. Why? Because He said so.

The sufferings of this day will cease to be and the coming of the Lord will bring that abundant life which Jesus promised. "... I have come that they may have life, and have it to the full" (John 10:10).

I am deeply moved when I think about the first followers of Jesus and how they must have felt at that time. Knowing that under their very eyes He was crucified, died, and was buried—then suddenly He was risen from the tomb!

Where do you stand on this? Do you believe this? Those of us who do believe should tell the Good News to everyone. If the good news of the lottery winners is so important, then why not make more important the most important news which is the Good News of Jesus Christ? Yes, we who are literally waiting on His return should come to our knees with loud praises and shouts. We should be living according to His teachings, so that we will not be strangers to Him when He comes. We should praise Him ever day.

A LAST WILL AND TESTAMENT COMPARISON

People use what is known as a Last Will and Testament. It is a covenant, agreement, or promise. Its purpose is fulfilled at the time of death of the deceased. Its contained promise is fulfilled through the courts of law.

God uses what is known as the New Testament. It is a covenant, agreement, or promise. Its purpose is fulfilled at the time of death of the sins of the sinner. Its contained promise is fulfilled through Christ Jesus.

If the last will and testament of your forgotten uncle revealed a mega-bucks inheritance, what would you be likely to do? *First,* you would have to hear the reading of the last will and testament. *Secondly,* when the announcement came that you would receive a huge inheritance, you would not be able to contain yourself. You would probably shout and tell everyone about it. A new joy of life would take over, and a new kind of happiness would find its place.

Let's compare this with God's New testament promise of our inheritance through Christ. *When you read and hear* what God is saying, you will know which inheritance is greater. Where your eyes see your uncle's inheritance, in contrast, your faith will allow you to see the inheritance that God has prepared for all who will believe in His Son.

Perhaps you have already had these two inheritances, one from a great uncle and one from God. Everything being equal, both testaments and promises having been written and read, which one is the greatest? Obviously, God's testament or promise. Why? Because the Gift of Life is infinite, and the uncle's inheritance is finite.

That which comes from God's estate is everlasting. This includes fellowship with the Son of the Living God and the Holy Spirit and all debts paid with God's guarantee of life eternal. This is truly "The Abundant Life."

CHAPTER 11

PRAYER

Almost everyone prays in some manner. They pray for someone else or for themselves. They may pray to images, false gods or to God Himself. Prayers are offered for a host of reasons. We see millions of Islam's praying on their knees. Prayer blankets are considered sacred to millions who religiously pray to God. We see pictures of Jews praying at the Wailing Wall in Jerusalem. "Wail" means to cry out in grief, sorrow, or lamentation. The book of Amos (5:16) reads, "Therefore this is what the Lord, the Lord God Almighty, says: There will be wailing in all the streets and cries of anguish in every public square..." We need to be more consistent in crying out to God individually and collectively. In doing so, we show our dependency upon God, and, more importantly, our love for Him. The apostle Paul said, "And my God will meet all your needs according to his glorious riches in Christ Jesus" (Philippians 4:19).

Prayer is having communion with God. Genuine prayer should always be preceded with praises and thanks for everything. God wants us to fellowship with Him through prayer in full faith. When we pray to God in reverence and thanksgiving, we honor Him. It is hard for us to understand just how much God loves us and wants us to talk with Him in prayer.

Praying for others is truly an act of love, which God honors. Prayers are most effective when we are spiritually prepared. Jesus helps us to understand these things. He tells us that if we live in Him and obey the Words of the Holy Bible, our prayers will be answered. Most people exercise prayer in a variety of ways. Prayer is the means by which we express ourselves before God. Prayer is first mentioned in the Bible in Genesis 4:26: "At that time men began to call upon the name of the Lord."

PRAYER—THE ANSWER TO MAN'S NEEDS

People of all races and nationalities pray to God. He is all knowing. God certainly knew a man called Job who deeply loved the

Lord. Job, a wealthy and godly man, lost all of his possessions. After many great trials and struggles he called out to God, saying, "I know that you can do all things; no plan of yours can be thwarted" (Job 42:2). Read about this man in the book of Job who was tested beyond imagination.

Prayer requires responsive faith. It is only through our faith that we can please God. Without faith, it is impossible to please God (Hebrews 11:6). Prayer is a sign of hope and a measure of faith. All people should pray because it is called of God. There is power in prayer because all things are possible with God. Vocalizing prayer keeps the mind awake and sharper..." The prayer of a righteous man is powerful and effective" (James 5:16). We must never feel we are not good enough to come to the Lord in prayer.

ACKNOWLEDGING GOD

Jeremiah the prophet lived during the latter part of the seventh century. He was a very sensitive man who loved his people. He heard the message from God, whom he acknowledged as, the one who made the earth and set it in place. He heard God say, "Call to me and I will answer you and tell you great and unsearchable things you do not know" (Jeremiah 33:3). Note that God asked Jeremiah to call upon Him. We learn a lesson from this passage in Jeremiah. God wants us to call on him.

UNDERSTANDING THE DEEPER SIDE
TO EFFECTIVE PRAYER

Though God hears everyone's prayers, it is very important to know how to pray to God effectively. All people who pray to God want God to hear and respond to their prayers. God has asked that men seek Him and His strength continually (1 Chronicles 16:11). He also said, in Proverbs 15:8 "...But the prayer of the upright pleases him." *Prayer has been established by God and for His purposes.*

Some people pray to God, but do not have a true relationship with His Son Jesus Christ who has been given all authority in heaven and earth. They may not trust or obey Him. *Fellowship with God requires believing in Jesus Christ. Believing means to trust, follow and obey.*

He is indispensable when it comes to having an intimate relationship with God the Father. Prayer has a distinct meaning and effectiveness when the conditions in the Holy Scriptures are met. Jesus said, "... Apart from me you can do nothing" (John 15:5).

ARE YOU DISENCHANTED WITH PRAYER?

When you pray, keep alert. Don't become dull and drowsy. We may become disenchanted with our prayer life simply because we haven't taken prayer seriously enough. There may be times when prayer doesn't seem to be doing what we think it should. It could be that we always expect God to react according to our terms. We must not give up. However, to be effective we should develop a consistency and dedication, and above all a faithful spirit. Consistency in our prayer life with a true faithfulness will please God. It might help if we consider that God wants everyone to lift up holy hands in prayer, without anger or disputing (1 Timothy 2:8).

GOD KNOWS OUR WEAKNESSES
AND HELPS US TO PRAY

Paul teaches us about the *One* who will help us when we don't know quite how to pray. "In the same way, the *Spirit* helps us in our weakness. We do not know what we ought to pray for, but the Spirit himself intercedes for us with groans that words cannot express" (Romans 8:26).

God invites us to call upon Him. He said in Psalms 50:15, "And call upon me in the day of trouble; I will deliver you, and you will honor me." God wants us to call upon Him in faith and, above all, in truth. Give an ear to what He says in Psalms 81:10: "... *Open your mouth wide and I will fill it.*" As you can see, we have no excuse now, do we? What a mighty God we serve!

JESUS GIVES US A GREAT SECRET TO PRAYER

Referred to as the "Master Key" to prayer, or better yet, the Master's Key, Jesus said, "If you remain in me and my words remain in you, ask whatever you wish, and it will be given you" (John 15:7). Observe carefully the two conditions which Jesus gives. First, "*If* you remain in me." Second, "*If* my Words remain in you." The word "*If*" places a dependent condition upon the promise. When and if this condition is met, we know we have followed Christ's instruction. Interestingly, if you truly live in the Word of God, you will be living in Christ.

Jesus also said, "If you obey my commands, you will remain in my love, just as I have obeyed my Father's commands and remain in his love" (John 15:10). When we keep His laws, we live in Him. It is the only way we can show our love. If we say, we love you Lord, and then don't follow His commands, we have a contradiction.

He said in John 14:23, "If anyone loves me, he will obey my teaching," and here's where we learn a great secret to our prayer life. *When we study His Word and then apply His Word in our daily living, we know that we will be living in Christ.*

MORE TEACHING ABOUT PRAYER
FROM THE LORD

The Savior of the world again helps us to pray. Jesus, when He was finishing His Sermon on the Mount said this about prayer. "Ask and it will be given to you; seek and you will find; knock and the door will be opened to you" (Matthew 7:7).

(1) "To ask" we must drop our human pride.
(2) "To seek" we know God will provide the answer.
(3) "To knock" we know that we came to God who loves us.

After Jesus' teaching upon asking, seeking, and knocking, He gave us something more to think about. He said, "Which of you, if his son asks for bread, will give him a stone? Or if he asks for a fish, will give him a snake? If you, then, though you are evil, know how to give good gifts to your children, how much more will your Father in heaven give good gifts to those who ask him!" (Matthew 7:9-11).

In the account presented by Mathew 6:5-15, Jesus was addressing His disciples. He taught them several things. First, He said, make your prayer private and personal to the Father. Secondly, don't pray with self-conceited empty words, because the Father already knows our

needs. Jesus tells us to find a quiet place, and to pray in secret to the Father.

ABOUT PRAYERS FOR OTHERS

Our prayers for others should be for their faith and commitment, their desire to minister to others, their boldness, spiritual understanding, strength, endurance, weaknesses, burdens, joys, and spiritual well being. Other suggested prayers should include the following. The President of our country, all of our nation's leaders, spiritual ministers working in other countries. Pray for those who place God's Word in all parts of the world, those who feed the poor, the weak, and hungry, the ministers in our local churches. Pray for their respective, outreach ministries, their spiritual and physical needs and their preaching and teaching agendas. Pray for those who care for the sick and the aged. And we must never forget those who are in prisons.

PRAYING WITH PRAYER PARTNERS

It is profitable to bring prayer partners into your Christian activities. There is power in doing so. Jesus said in Matthew 18:19, "Again, I tell you that if two of you on earth agree about anything you ask for, it will be done for you by my Father in heaven." When is the last time you called upon some friend to pray with you?

DIFFERENT KINDS OF PRAYERS

There are prayers of worship, confession, adoration, praise, and thanksgiving. Prayers for others are very necessary in our Christian walk. The Lord's Prayer helps us shape our own words and petitions as we present them before the Father.

REVIEWING THE LORD'S PRAYER (Matthew 6:9-13)
(To help new converts who have not prayed this prayer)

As you read the Lord's prayer typed in capital letters below, meditate on its meaning. To help you, read the meaning given in the small letters.

OUR FATHER, (To acknowledge God with praise, as our heavenly and eternal God).

IN HEAVEN, (To realize there is a heaven.)

HALLOWED BE YOUR NAME, (To honor His name.)

YOUR KINGDOM COME, (To invite His righteousness, peace and joy in the Holy Spirit.)

YOUR WILL BE DONE ON EARTH AS IT IS IN HEAVEN. (To show submissiveness and dependency upon His will.)

GIVE US TODAY OUR DAILY BREAD. (To ask God for daily spiritual and physical needs for our sustaining.)

FORGIVE US OUR DEBTS, AS WE ALSO HAVE FORGIVEN OUR DEBTORS. (To ask for His forgiveness for our wrongs, as we contemplate forgiving others for the wrongs done to us. God's forgiveness does not depend upon our forgiving others. This warning though helps us see the need to forgive others.)

AND LEAD US NOT INTO TEMPTATION, BUT DELIVER US FROM THE EVIL ONE. (Not to imply that God leads us into temptation, but asking God's help in overcoming sin.)

FOR THINE IS THE KINGDOM, AND THE POWER, AND THE GLORY, FOREVER. AMEN. (Is to acknowledge God's righteousness, His sovereignty, His almightiness, and His character and ultimate authority.) *Note*: This passage is part of verse 13 and is quoted from the King James version. It is included here because most, if not all Protestant churches use the King James version when praying the Lord's prayer. It is not included in the New International version. Other than this partial verse, all other Bible verses in this book are from the New International version.

AMEN. Simply means, "So be it."

FIRST TIME EVER TO CALL GOD "FATHER"

Believers of Jesus Christ received the right to call God, "Father," for the first time in history when Jesus taught us the Lord's prayer. This is a distinct privilege we have, not only to call God "Father," but

131

also to use the very Words of Christ to help us pray to God (Matthew 6:9-15).

GOD'S CALL TO GOD'S PEOPLE

"If my people, which are called by my name, shall humble themselves and pray, and seek my face, and turn away from their wicked ways; then will I hear from heaven, and will forgive their sin, and will heal their land" (2 Chronicles 7:14). We see here God's call for our prayers, which demand a humble spirit before praying. In this passage God says, "I will hear." This should give us an even deeper confidence and faith in our future prayers. Prayer should be considered a privilege and not a ritual. *Praying should not be considered a penalty, as it is a distinct privilege.* Faith is necessary in one's prayer life because it shows trust in God, and He will honor this. "Now faith is being sure of what we hope for and certain of what we do not see" (Hebrews 11:1).

WHAT TO EXPECT FROM GOD

This very moment God is listening to millions of prayers in all languages and dialects. He has understanding of each one. We should be thankful for immediate access and no waiting lines to come to Him. God is able to respond in His own way and in His own time, although we often expect Him to respond immediately. It is equally important to know that God may be answering our prayers in a way that we do not understand. *His wisdom is more than all of the grains of sand upon the beaches of the world.* Jesus said, "And I will do whatever you ask in my name, so that the Son may bring glory to the Father. You may ask me for anything in my name, and I will do it" (John 14:13). The Word itself tells us what we can expect from God.

THE HOLY SPIRIT HELPS IN DIFFICULT TIMES

God has made provisions through the Scriptures to help us in our prayer lives. This is one reason why reading the Bible is so important, because we learn many things. When we are faced with problems or situations and don't know what to pray for, God will be with us. The Holy Spirit will intercede for us and will pray in our behalf, in ways which we cannot express, before God (Romans 8:26). God will then respond in His divine ways which will satisfy and bring peace. Remember, praying in the name of Jesus Christ bring honor and glory to God.

WHAT DOES GOD EXPECT FROM US?

First, there is faith. First John 5:4 tells us, as children of God, we are able to defeat the hard times in our lives through our faith. *If you pray by faith, then you can expect God to respond.* It is His rule. God says we are to ask in faith and not waver or tremble (James 1:6). He expects our devoted attention when we pray and does not want us to become lethargic or slumberous. Posture in prayer may depend upon the occasion and place. A ready mind shows respect for God. Many people say, "Oh! I wish this or that would happen." Wishing cannot be compared to a true faith in the God of all creation. When He says, "Trust in the Lord forever, for the Lord, is the Rock eternal," then trust in the Lord (Isaiah 26:4). He means what he says. To trust means to depend on, or to expect. To wish means to long to have something. With God, we can truly expect a reaction to our prayers. God would not ask us to trust in Him if He did not plan to carry out what He says.

WHEN DOES PRAYER BEGIN AND END?

We learn from the third chapter of Ecclesiastes that there is a time for everything. A time for birth, death, planting, pulling, healing, mourning, love, hate, silence and talking, and many other things. In a like manner there is a time for formal prayers, corporate prayers, worship prayers, confession prayers, adoration prayers, thanksgiving prayers, and intercession prayers. Other than these kinds of prayers, the steadfast Christian should be in communion with God every minute of the day. *When does prayer begin and end?* As often as you want it to. Anyone who lives in Christ knows that their interchange or prayer life with God has no ending. Sin definitely separates us from God: it breaks our fellowship with Him. The Christian can re-establish his fellowship with God by confessing his sins. Then, he may quickly get back into prayer with God. It should be remembered that when a believer comes to God with a repentant heart, and confess their sins, God, who is faithful and just will forgive his sins. Jesus paid for our sins at the cross. Believing this, and believing in His resurrection is what has brought us into God's righteousness in the first place.

GOD IS WITH HIS OWN

God constantly sees and hears us. King David, in praising God said, "If I go up to the heavens, you are there; if I make my bed in the depths, you are there" (Psalms 139:8). We are always in the presence of God. We cannot escape Him whether we are good or bad, right or wrong. We may choke off our fellowship through our improprieties, but not our relationship. As Christians, we know that sin breaks our fellowship with God, but it does not change our relationship with God. In this next passage, John the apostle said, "My dear children, I write this to you so that you will not sin. But if anybody does sin, we have one who speaks to the Father in our defense — Jesus Christ, the Righteous One. He is the atoning sacrifice for our sins, and not only ours but also for the sins of the whole world" 1 John 2:1,2).

"FOR HE LIVES WITH YOU"

We must not limit ourselves before God. He does not limit Himself to the believer. Why? Because the believer has already been given the gift of the Holy Spirit. Perhaps this is where we fall short in our understanding. To clear this up, let us re-read this next passage very carefully because these are the very words of Jesus, in John 14:15,17. "If you love me, you will obey what I command. And I will ask the Father, and he will give you another Counselor to be with you forever—the Spirit of truth. The world cannot accept him, because it neither sees him nor knows him. *But you know him, for he lives with you and will be in you."*

Do you think that Jesus, who was God in the flesh, would say such a thing and not mean it? When we take the time to read God's Word, we come to know what God Himself is saying, as these things were written for our learning.

SCRIPTURES TO MEDITATE UPON WHEN PRAYING

"If you believe, you will receive whatever you ask for in prayer" (Matthew 21:22).

134

"Dear friends, if our hearts do not condemn us, we have confidence before God and receive from him anything we ask, because we obey his commands and do what pleases him" (1 John 3:21, 22).

"He will call upon me, and I will answer him; I will be with him in trouble, I will deliver him, and honor him" (Psalms 91:15).

"Carry each other's burdens, and in this way you will fulfill the law of Christ" (Galatians 6:2).

Jesus said, "... My house will be called a house of prayer" (Matthew 21:13).

The early church "Joined all together constantly in prayer..." (Acts 1:14).

"And the prayer offered in faith will make the sick person well" (James 5:15).

THINGS TO THINK ABOUT WHEN PRAYING

God responds to the prayers of the destitute (Psalms 102:17).

Don't worry; instead, present your requests to God (Philippians 4:6).

God's ears are attentive to the prayers of the righteous (1 Peter 3:12).

Let nothing hinder our prayers (1 Peter 3:7).

Pray for those in authority (1 Timothy 2:1-2).

Stay clear minded and self-controlled so that you can pray (1 Peter 4:7).

I am a man of prayer (Psalms 109:4).

Pray for one another (James 5:16).

Pray continually (1 Thessalonians 5:17).

The Holy Spirit helps us to pray (Romans 8:26).

LESSONS WE LEARN

Aside from the many reported times that Jesus prayed, we could correctly assume that Jesus was continually in prayer with the Father. And so it should be the same with believers. For the true follower of Christ, prayer should not only be used on occasion, but it should be continual. We may not have to be saying something, or asking for something to be in continual prayer. When Paul told those at Thessalonica to "Pray unceasingly" continually, I'm sure he did not intend for them to be on their knees around the clock. To pray in continuance means we maintain an attitude of prayer. This allows us to shoot arrow prayers or short prayers up to God when the occasion arises. When we maintain a godlike attitude we will experience God's presence. Then we are able to maintain a spiritual relationship which will lead us to specific prayers of appreciation, worship, intercession and needs for others.

When we pray in a private setting, also called closet praying, we are better able to establish an intimacy with God through Jesus Christ. However, we must always remember that we are not on our own because the Holy Spirit lives in every believer. [See Holy Spirit given to believers in John 14:26].

"PRAY THAT YOU WILL NOT FALL INTO TEMPTATION"

He asked the disciples to pray just shortly before Judas betrayed Him. He said, "Pray that you will not fall into temptation" (Luke 22:40). He then asked them to pray a second time so that they would not fall into temptation (Luke 22:46). *We learn an important lesson from these passages.* When we are in communion with God, it is hard to fall into temptation. So, when you are tempted, pray to God, and temptation will leave you. His instruction to the disciples to pray was perhaps given to them because Jesus knew that His disciples would be faced with the trials of life even after He was taken away. Jesus knew they would scatter and deny Him and would need Divine strength. Prayer brings with it Divine blessings and power. There is power in prayer.

Aside from a complete and full surrender to Jesus Christ and the command, "to love one another", prayer is the most powerful and fulfilling act given to God's faithful people. Prayers bring glory to God when prayed with faith, and in the name of His Son, Jesus Christ. It allows God to show His love, and it brings results that could not be accomplished otherwise.

Thanks be to God for the blessing of prayer!

CHAPTER 12

THE CHURCH

The Church is the living and the deceased who have been redeemed by the blood of Christ through their individual affirmation of Christ's bloody death and His glorious resurrection. They are the ones who have been added into the one Body of Jesus Christ (Acts 2:41). The Holy Bible refers to them as the saved, disciples, believers, saints, and Christians (Acts 2:47, John 15:8, John 17:20, Romans 1:7, Acts 11:26).

The saved are spread all over the world and are found in many denominations and local bodies. Those who have been redeemed by the blood of Christ have been saved by God's grace through the Word of God. The saved are the church and they are kept by the Holy Spirit (John 14:17). It is a great blessing to be united with the spiritual body of God's people. They are the ones who have been sanctified or set apart, and have been reconciled to God (1 Corinthians 6:11).

The Church is the collective body of those who have believed and those who *will yet* come to believe in the birth, death, and resurrection of Jesus Christ. Jesus Christ is coming back for this Church. Local churches are those who make up the larger or corporate body of the Church.

The Church has many functions. It has been given its greatest challenge by the Lord Jesus, which is to love one another. Its objective comes also from the Lord Jesus Christ who said, "All authority in heaven and on earth has been given to me. Therefore go and make disciples of all nations, baptizing them in the name of the Father and of the Son and of the Holy Spirit, and teaching them everything I have commanded you. And surely I am with you always, to the very end of the age" (Matthew 28:18-20).

The Church preaches the Word, and, when people truly hear the message of God, they are then added to the Church. Christ died for the Church and gave to His followers the ministry of reconciliation. The Church, being a spiritual body, operates properly when it is fully led by the Holy Spirit. Let us begin with Jesus as He spoke to his disciple Peter. "And I tell you that you are Peter, and on this rock I will build my church, and the gates of Hades will not overcome it" (Matthew 16:18). For many, it is not easy to grasp the true meaning of what Jesus said. However, when we begin to understand His words, we begin to see the Church in a whole new and different light. Why? Because His words are truth and their meaning, represent the foundation truth of our religion.

Religion that is not based upon the doctrine of Jesus Christ is false. *The true doctrine of Jesus Christ is centered in both teaching and believing that He was both God and man, and that His one-time sacrifice and resurrection brings salvation through faith.* The true Church is built upon this truth. To understand the deeper inside meaning, we must be willing to release the exterior images about the church which most of us have developed over time. These exterior images keep us from the truth of what the church really is and what it means. What are these images? They are those things that have erroneously led too many astray through tradition, time, and false teaching.

Some continue to think of the Church as a building for public worship. Some look at the Church as a place to hold a religious service. Some use the church building as a place for social gathering. *Some have made it a system of religion,* and some merely think of it as a place to go to on Sundays. This is not what Jesus meant when He said, "I will build my church." Let's move into the true meaning of what Jesus said.

THE CHURCH'S FOUNDATION

The Church is built upon truth. Jesus said to Peter, "Upon this rock I will build my church." We know that Jesus Christ is that rock, the truth, and through His Blood sacrifice we who believe will have life forever. Because Jesus told Peter, "And I will give unto thee the keys of the kingdom of heaven," we know that Peter was charged to preach the Good News of Jesus Christ. It was in his first sermon that three thousand people were saved and received the Holy Spirit.

These people then continued to learn of Christ. With one another, they continued praying together. They broke bread and continued to remember what Jesus had done at the cross They kept praising Him for His great sacrifice and atoning work at the cross. This breaking of bread is what we do today in our Communion services. Christ's broken body and shed blood is what we continue to remember when we receive the host in a most holy- communion (Luke 22:19).

ABOUT THE CHURCH

According to the written Word, there is no other way, and there is no other name under heaven given for us to be reconciled to God other than the name of Jesus Christ., "For other foundation can no man lay than that is laid, which is Jesus Christ" (1 Corinthians 3:11).

> The Church has a Head, which is Christ.
> The Church has a Groom, which is Christ.
> The Church has a Bride, they are, the Redeemed.
> Its origin is God.
> Its source is Christ.
> Its power is the Holy Spirit.
> Its headquarters is Heaven.
> Faith holds it together.
> Sin hinders its mission.

The goal of the Church —

♦ **Remain** as one in Christ's love. (John 17:20,21,22)

♦ **Preserve** the stewardship of the Gospel. (2 Corinthians 5:18,19)

♦ **Feed** the church of God which the Holy Spirit made us overseers, maintain sound Biblical doctrine by rightly dividing the word of truth at all times (2 Timothy 2:15, Acts 20:28).

Jesus gave His Church its Great Commission, which in itself should keep us all busy until He comes again. True believers in all denominations should recognize their true brethren wherever they are—this honors Christ. Things which pull apart God's people, such as arguments over words and feelings, can be replaced with the truth of the Word, and, above all, by the love of Christ.

ONE PERFECT SACRIFICE

"For Christ did not enter a man-made sanctuary that was only a copy of the true one; he entered heaven itself, now to appear for us in God's presence. Nor did he enter into heaven to offer himself again and again, the way the high priest enters the Most Holy Place every year with blood that is not his own" (Hebrews 9:24-25). This sin offering, under the Mosaic Law, is what the Jews were practicing even when Christ was on this earth.

"How much more, then, will the blood of Christ, who through the eternal Spirit offered himself unblemished to God, cleanse our conscience from acts that lead to death, so that we may serve the living God!" (Hebrews 9:14). Those who serve the living God today are those who have been sanctified, set apart, and are truly the members of the true Church of God. *There is only one Church, many denominations, but only one Church. This is the Church He is coming back for.*

THE CHURCH'S BEGINNING

Christianity began on the day of Pentecost. Believers were first called Christians at Antioch (Acts 11:26). Upon believing and following the person of Jesus Christ through our word testimony and behavior, we know that we are the ones who Jesus prayed for in John 17:20. "My prayer is not for them alone [His disciples]. I pray also for those [all future believers] who will believe in me through their message." This refers to how we act and what we tell others about Christ.

JESUS EXPLAINS THE CHURCH

It was immediately after Jesus strongly reprimanded the Jews for using the Temple as a market that He said, "Destroy this temple, and I will raise it again in three days" (John 2:19). Though Jesus was talking about the Temple of His Body, they did not understand anything about what Jesus was saying. Their thoughts were focused on their visible temple or synagogue, knowing it took them forty-six years to build. Jesus was talking about spiritual things and because of their arrogance, they could not see the truth of what Jesus was saying.

The "Temple of His Body" which Jesus was talking about was His Body. The Jews were blind to this truth. They were locked into their own religious ideas through pride. Pride never lets us see the truth. *We come into Christ's Body through a spiritual change called "conversion"* (Acts 3:19). Then, our body becomes the live in temple for God's Spirit (1 Corinthians 3:16). "...unless you change and become like little children you will never enter the Kingdom of Heaven", said Jesus (Matthew 18:3).

Formation of the early church and its evangelistic and missionary work and what has been happening in the universal church today are not the same. The exception are those who continue in the true doctrine of Christ. The building, that Jesus mentioned, was not intended to mean the erection of church buildings of glorious architecture, which please the minds of men. He did not intend for the Church to be used for political dominance, power, and profit, or even social settings. His bloody, bodily sacrifice and atoning death, and God the Father's intent, was something much deeper and momentous than that. Jesus cleansed the Temple when He saw it used for the wrong reasons. "He said, "It is written, My house will be called a house of prayer, but you are making it a den of robbers" (Matthew 21:13).

JESUS SENDS THE HOLY SPIRIT
AND THE CHURCH BEGINS

After telling the disciples to wait upon the Holy Spirit, whom He would send, Jesus ascended into heaven. After Jesus ascended into Heaven, He sent the Holy Spirit to where they were waiting. The Holy Spirit's arrival came with a noise from the sky that sounded like a strong wind blowing (Acts 2:1,2). The Holy Spirit came into their hearts and they began to speak in other languages. There were some men from other countries nearby, who, upon hearing the noise became excited and thought the people were drunk. Peter reminded them of what the Prophet Joel said. "And it shall come to pass in the last days, saith God, I will pour out of my Spirit upon all flesh..." (Acts 2:17). The "final days" began with this account in Acts, and will end when Christ returns. [The main theme of the book of Acts is the history and development of the early church]. The early Church began with the Apostles. This would bring glory and honor to God the Father and Jesus Christ through the

142

building of the Church, which would become known as the Christian Church. Actually, when Jesus said, it is finished, His Church began.

PETER'S FIRST SERMON A LESSON FOR US...SIMPLICITY

Again, we mention Peter and his first sermon. The preached word is clear and uncomplicated. Peter told the Israelites that they and all of Israel should know that this Jesus, whom they crucified, was the one that God sent—their Messiah. Deeply troubled they asked Peter what they should do. Peter just preached the Gospel of Christ. They that heard him, repented, and became the first three thousand new converts in Christ's Church. Being filled with the Holy Spirit, they became joyous to know that Jesus forgave them even after they took part in His crucifixion. People of this day are no different. Why? Because it was your sins and mine that took part in Christ's crucifixion? Is Jesus Christ your Messiah, your Savior? The lesson we should learn from Peter lies in the truth and simplicity of the Gospel: all have sinned and need a Savior.

In many churches today we see folks gather on Sundays and perhaps feel good about having gone to a church service. I have heard it said from dedicated pastors that only small parts of their church people are saved. Who is at fault? Is the preaching correct, or is it that people want religion and not salvation? Let's face the truth—first you get saved, then religion follows. "Not everyone who says to Me, Lord, Lord, shall enter the kingdom of Heaven," said Jesus in Matthew 7:21.

Building the Church means adding to the Body of Christ, the saved. Building the Church means growing together in the Word of God. Remember, where the preacher is one who preaches salvation and Christian living according to God's Word, he is also the one whom God has chosen to shepherd God's flock. At judgment time, when the unbelievers face judgment, they will not be able to blame the pastor. We are all charged with building Christ's Church.

GIFTS TO THE CHURCH

The appointment of Christ's Disciples would provide a means for future followers to perpetuate the Church of Jesus Christ. Subsequent men and women then would carry on the work of the Church; the Church's preparation through holy living would make herself ready for the day when Christ, the Groom, would return for His Bride, the Church. *Even as God had chosen Moses to be a leader of the Israelites, and the disciples to carry on the work of the gospel of Christ, believers of today are charged with the work associated with the gospel.* The Pastor, the evangelist, the elders, and deacons, are charged with a holy work. Ephesians 4:11 tells us about special gifts given. "It was he who gave some to be apostles, some to be prophets, some to be evangelists, and some to be pastors and teachers." Christians, though, are charged by God to tell the good news of salvation to all who are not yet saved.

"Now to each one the manifestation of the Spirit is given for the common good. To one there is given through the Spirit the message of wisdom, to another the message of knowledge by means of the same Spirit, *to another faith* by the same Spirit, to another gifts of healing by that one Spirit, to another miraculous powers, to another prophecy, to another distinguishing between spirits, to another speaking in different kinds of tongues, and to still another the interpretation of tongues. All these are the work of one and the same Spirit, and he gives them to each one, just as he determines" (1 Corinthians 12:7-11).

TAKING CHRIST'S CHURCH SERIOUSLY

God gives different gifts to believers for His own purposes. Christians are to mature in their faith if they want to serve God effectively. Paul said, "I became a servant of this gospel by the gift of God's grace given me through the working of His power" (Ephesians 3:7).

This next passage teaches us more about God's gifts to us—both grace and faith. "For it is by *grace* you have been saved, through *faith*—and this not from yourselves, it is the gift of God..." (Ephesians 2:8). We see here two gifts given at the same time, grace, and faith. *Grace* gives the believer the power to do God's will. *Faith* when used with self-control will result in actions and will make our faith complete by what we do with it (James 2:22).

144

In regard to grace, "His divine power has given us everything we need for life and godliness through our knowledge of him who called us by his own glory and goodness" (2 Peter 1:3). *Saving faith* is given to all who come to Christ. To some, an added gift of faith is given by the Holy Spirit to be used for God's purposes (1 Corinthians 12:9). Believers are encouraged to do more with their faith by working it. (See faith chapter)

BEES AND THE CHRISTIAN

The church needs to work with its faith in the same way honey bees work with their tongues. They produce honey and they also gather pollen and pollinate other plants they visit. Christians should carry their faith with their tongues and pollinate non-believers with the gospel of Christ. Even as bees are consistently busy with their God assigned work, Christians should be busy with their God assigned work [Matthew 28:19]. How about you, when is the last time you went pollinating? God has given His believers different kinds of gifts to build up His Body.

THE CHURCH A SPIRITUAL BODY

The church that Jesus said He would build in three days is a divine spiritual body which is set apart from any other body. Christ died for His Church which is the body, the redeemed. He brought honor and glory to God when He suffered and died for it. Then, beginning with the Apostles, and through them, He expects continuity in our works. Every believer has responsibility and accountability in the works of the Church through a working of our faith. Are you really taking seriously the work He has given you in the ministry of reconciliation? Is your faith working to bring glory to God?

ABOUT TITHING

Tithe means to give a tenth of our income for the support of the church and its many mission outreaches. Leviticus 27:30 reveals giving "A tithe of everything from the land, whether grain from the soil or fruit from the trees, belongs to the Lord; *it is holy to the Lord.*" Abraham gave God a tenth of everything (Genesis 14:20). Should we tithe today? Many Christians give a tenth of everything they earn for the storehouse of God *knowing through their faith* God's work is being completed in all parts of the world. The Lord speaks to us in Malachi 3:10. He says, "Bring the whole tithe into the storehouse, that there may be food in my house. *Test me in this,* says the Lord Almighty, and see if I will not throw open the floodgates of heaven and pour out so much blessing that you will not have room enough for it." Keep your motive right and God will richly bless you. Proverbs 3:9-10 gives us great advice on this subject of giving back to God what He has given us in the first place. It says, "Honor the Lord with your wealth, with the first-fruits of all your crops; then your barns will be filled to overflowing..." The Bible speaks for itself. God has given you His clarification. "Each man should give what he has decided in his heart to give, not reluctantly or under compulsion, for God loves a cheerful giver" (2 Corinthians 9:7).

CHRISTIANS ARE TO USE THEIR TALENTS

Christians should make Jesus *"All In All."* Having each been given a gift from God, we are expected to use our individual talents to help achieve perfection in the fellowship of the church. When this is accomplished, a specific firmness in the spirit of the Church is fulfilled, and in this way, Christ is edified. When the church departs from His teachings and loses its first love for Christ, the entire body deviates from its purpose, to grow in grace (Ephesians 4:10-13). Some believers do their best work when they just lift up and help those who work ever so silently in the church.

TRUE MEANING AND PURPOSE OF THE CHURCH

God, wanting to bring man back to Himself, did something which no human being can do. He sent His only Son to the face of this earth to sacrifice Himself upon a cross. Those who would believe in the meaning of this sacrifice would become reconciled to God. Then, God gave the ministry of reconciliation to those who would believe in His Son's birth, death, and resurrection. What is the ministry of reconciliation? It is a command from God, to all of God's people, to prepare and present the message of Christ to the entire world. God chose to have all believers take part in His Divine plan of salvation. God's written record found in 2 Corinthians 5:18-19 says, "All this is from God, who reconciled us to Himself through Christ and *gave us the ministry of reconciliation;* that God was reconciling the world to himself in Christ, not counting men's sins against them. And he has committed to us [all believers] the message of reconciliation." To reconcile means to restore to harmony.

God charges every Christian with telling non-Christians how they too can be redeemed and delivered from the bondage of sin and its consequence. When used with prayer and preparation through the Word of God, the Christian is enabled through the Holy Spirit to bring others to Christ. Christians who are prepared from the pulpits and who study God's Word become instruments of God in this holy work.

Nothing can take the place of the written Word. When it is preached, or when it is used by the Christian to tell others why Jesus died and why He was raised from the dead, many will become reconciled to God. There is great power when we call upon the Holy Spirit and use the words of Scripture as we witness. Peter gives us an example of this great power. "While Peter was still speaking these words, *the Holy Spirit came on all who heard the message"* (Acts 10:44).

The Church began with the spilled blood of Jesus Christ (Acts 20:28). It continues to grow through Christians who continue to obey Christ's command to help others become reconciled to Christ. God the Father was manifested in His Son Jesus, who purchased the Church with His one-time blood sacrifice. Now there is a pardon, for all who believe the Gospel of Christ. Those who come to accept and believe in Jesus Christ will, through divine illumination and manifestation, take part in His death and resurrection, and become a part of the church. They are God's elect who are referred to in the Scriptures as the Church of God, the flock, or His sheep.

His words, "And the gates of Hades will not overcome it" means that nothing would ever change what Jesus was about to do. The truth that can never be changed is Jesus Christ. He is the One, "Who gave himself as a ransom for all men" (1 Timothy 2:6). He is the only mediator between man and God (1 Timothy 2:5). Those who will believe in the redemptive work of Christ, without proof, take on a new spiritual life which is acceptable to God, and are then added to the Church. We must remember that believing in Christ becomes real when we trust in Him and obediently follow His teachings.

GOD IS ALL IN ALL
WHEN IT COMES TO CHRISTIAN SERVICE

God gives the increase to those things that His servants will do. "So neither he who plants nor he who waters is anything, *but only God* who makes things grow. The man who plants and the man who waters have one purpose, and each will be rewarded according to his own labor" (1 Corinthians 3:7-8).

As we review what Paul said to the Corinthians, calling them "worldly" or walking according to the sinful nature, they remained only as babes in Christ. Paul, through this account, is teaching us to grow in our service to God by being filled with the Holy Spirit. The Spirit cannot fill us very much when we continue to sin, although our sinning may not be deliberate. Sin must instantly be confessed. The gift of the Holy Spirit is given to every new believer. To have this gift means that His presence and power is available to believers. The believer, then, through faith, is able to testify for Jesus Christ and must continually strive to keep from sin. The believer has been freed from any judgment of his sins [Romans 8:1-2], but not freed from temptation. *However, do not let that hinder your service to God.* God gives believers His Spirit to enable them to draw upon His power to overcome sin so that the work of the church go unhindered.

In Ephesians 5:15-18, Paul says, "Be very careful, then, how you live—not as unwise but as wise, making the most of every opportunity, because the days are evil. Therefore do not be foolish, but understand what the Lord's will is for you. Do not get drunk on wine, which leads to debauchery (excessive indulgence of the appetites). *Instead, be filled with the Spirit."* Many fail to draw upon what God has already given them when they became saved. They fail to yield to the Spirit which God gave them (See Acts 10:44).

CHRISTIAN SERVICE BEING MADE FRUITFUL

Believers are to "Submit to one another out of reverence for

Christ" (Ephesians 5:21). "Those controlled by the sinful nature cannot please God," said Paul in Romans 8:8. Paul also said, *"Therefore, brothers,* we have an obligation—but it is not to the sinful nature, to live according to it. For if you live according to the sinful nature, you will die; but if by the Spirit you put to death the misdeeds of the body, you will live" (Romans 8:12,13). The believer's obligation is to live a life without sin so that he can worship and serve God with a clean heart. It is not possible to serve sin and God at the same time.

When the true doctrine of Jesus Christ is preached, and lived up to, the Holy Spirit will lead us into victory as we serve Him and worship Him. We must always remember that our service is not to ourselves, but to God. The church is to worship God in Spirit and truth, preach the Word, and always be ready to reach out into the world for the lost.

Let's try to see the church from God's perspective, and try to offset the image most of us have learned through time and traditions. The real and true church, which Jesus talked about to Peter, is not found in any system of religion which is apart from the authorized Scriptures. Man's philosophies, ideologies, and doctrines are useless. *The church, which Jesus said he would raise in three days, is the Temple of His Body.* To make an entrance into His sacred Body or His church, one must in truth believe upon His resurrection from the dead. Faith gets you in and the Holy Spirit guarantees your stay, *if the Spirit lives in you.* (Read Romans 10:8-10, Ephesians 2:8, 2 Corinthians 5:5.)

The church, being the collective body of God's people is kept by God's power through faith (1 Peter 1:5). They are the ones who have been converted from unbelievers to believers and followers of Jesus Christ. They are the ones who have been justified (Acts 13:39), and sanctified, or set apart by God (Hebrews 10:10).

The words "church and religion" are generally used or accepted as synonymous terms, yet they differ when it comes to their spiritual meaning and application. *Religion,* according to Webster, is defined as the service and adoration of God or a god as expressed in forms of worship and a way of life. Also, any one of the systems of faith and worship.

149

Church, according to John 2:21, which Jesus was talking about to Peter, is unerring in the singularity of a body, and this Body is unlike any other body, because it is the Body of Jesus Christ. And, when anyone becomes a believer, their body becomes the live in temple for the Holy Spirit (1 Corinthians 6:19).

The intent of this chapter on the Church is to help bring about an awareness of its Spiritual meaning and God's intention. Some look at the Church as a building for public religious worship and financial profit. In some churches, tradition with no Biblical purpose has been set in place in subtle ways over a long period. Many have grown to be quite complex and seemingly unchangeable. Some of these traditions have given us a false perception of the true meaning of the Church. A single example of this is found in acts of piety, or unchallenged authority, which is set in place by the hierarchy in some of our local churches. Varied interpretations of the Scriptures go unchallenged. Meaningless traditions must be replaced with a true ministry of reconciliation and the teaching of the law of love, which should dominate and permeate the church setting.

The church began with Christ; He commanded His disciples to build up the church through baptism. This spiritual baptism unites a believer with Jesus Christ, through the grace of God, to a new life which is everlasting. *The life of the Body should grow in the love of Christ in a true worship and a true stewardship of its many gifts.*

THE CHURCH IS CHARGED WITH THE FOLLOWING
  (1) Make known God's love. (John 3:16)
  (2) Love one another. (John 15:12)
  (3) Teach and preach. (Ephesians 4:11)
  (4) Edify the body of Christ. (Ephesians 4:12)
  (5) Remember His Body and Blood. (Luke 22:19-20)
  (6) Baptize new believers. (Matthew 28:19-20)
  (7) Feed the church of God. (Acts 20:28)
  (8) Keep the Holy Scriptures intact, neither adding, nor diminishing from its ownership or truth. (Rev 22:19, Deut. 4:2)

THE COST OF DISCIPLESHIP

Many today want to take part in the church but fail, because true purpose and commitment are absent. The cost of true religion requires one to bear his cross and follow Christ. There is a cost in following the Master, and He gives explicit instruction in Luke 14:25-35. He says, in principle, unless our motive is unselfish and we are willing to abandon things such as social status, wealth, or popularity for the purpose of ego and self esteem, we cannot be His disciples. Following Christ as a member of His church is not trouble free. To be involved in unloving attitudes or any behavior unbecoming a Christian is to continue to live a life in sin. These sins keep believers from serving God.

VIRTUE OF THE CHRISTIAN FAMILY

Excellence is the goal for the Christian and it takes dedication, commitment, and practice. It does not come without the giving of oneself in any situation or condition. *Correct action, thinking, and a Christ-like character must be the prevailing source for service.* God's effective power is available to the believer through the Holy Spirit's presence. The Christian who practices the presence of God has a distinct edge. Christians who follow Christ's words receive a great blessing. These promises of Christ apply to every person who will come to Him.

Living in Christ does not mean we will always understand all things. "And we know that in all things God works for the good of those who love him, who have been called according to his purpose" (Romans 8:28). Altruism, unselfish acts of love, in its purest form needs to be nurtured within the congregations.

PAUL EXPRESSES CONCERN WITH DIVISION IN THE CHURCH

Paul said to those at the Church in the city of Corinth, "Brothers, I could not address you as spiritual but as worldly—mere infants in Christ. I gave you milk, not solid food, for you were not ready for it. Indeed, you are still not ready. You are still worldly. For since there is jealousy and quarreling among you, are you not worldly? Are you not acting like mere men?" For when one says, I follow Paul, and another, I follow Apollos, Are you not mere men?" (1 Corinthians 3:1-4).

Paul reminded these believers of his calling in the work of the church. He then challenged those who would continue to build Christ's church (and this includes believers of today) to use only the true doctrine of Jesus Christ. Paul was concerned with anything which could bring division in the church. Church guardians of today should also be on the watch for the early signs of division in the church.

THE ROLE OF THE CHURCH

This may be disturbing and shocking news, but the *church does not save* anyone. We are saved by *God's grace through faith,* and not by anything which we may try to do on our own. However, the church has a distinct role in God's redemptive work and also the believer's behavior and lifestyle. Christians should come to know exactly what God's Word has to say about respective roles for individual believers and the church as whole. True believers should not be strangers to one another because they belong to the same household of God. What does this mean? It means that we stand together, on the foundation of what the apostles and the prophets have given us in both the Old and the New Testament. It means that the church is not built on any ideas of men or their philosophies but on the Word of God. The true test of our religion is based upon the written Word of God. God's first commandment must be placed ahead of our own agendas in everything we do. We must show and give honor to God through loud praises for His unconditional love and Grace, in every church service. We should acknowledge His Word much more than any ritual or tradition.

YOUR SERVICE IN HIS CHURCH

"Be shepherds of God's flock that is under your care, serving as overseers—not because you must, but because you are willing, as God wants you to be; not greedy for money, but eager to serve" (1 Peter 5:2). Preparation through the Holy Word and dedication to carry out God's wishes is the only way to serve the Lord Scripturally. God's Word says, "Do your best to present yourself to God as one approved, a workman who does not need to be ashamed and who correctly handles the word of truth"(2 Timothy 2:15).

DISCIPLINE IN THE CHURCH

Paul, disciple and follower of Christ, spoke very harshly to those at Corinth. He said something to them that is very much prevalent in some of our churches today. Addressing the Church of Corinth, Paul was trying to take action upon quarreling, jealousy, hot tempers, selfishness, insults, gossip, pride, and disorder. As one trying his best to help solve their problems and as an emissary of Christ, he felt their disapproval of what he was trying to do. He said we speak, as Christ would have us speak. He was referring to Titus, whom Paul had sent at another time. He mentioned to them that this was his third attempt at solving the problem, and if he had to come to them again personally, it would not go without punishment to those who had sinned.

At a different setting, Paul's close associate, and friend in Christ, Titus, told those at the Church at Corinth to do things which are good and useful and avoid stupid arguments and fights about the law? He said, give the heretic, a dissenter from orthodox belief, two warnings, then reject him. Perhaps at this point you grasp the situation very well. You may not agree with the strictness and authority displayed by both Paul and Titus, but, remember one thing, these accounts God had recorded for our admonition, and will give us the courage and strength to take a deeper interest in the truth and all matters about our own local church. (Read 2 Corinthians 12:11-21 and Chapter 13:1-11.)

When a sinful act is committed within the Church, a scriptural search for appropriate action should be taken. In Matthew 18:15-20, Jesus tells how things should done. He says the grievance must be addressed and an attempt should be made to settle the dispute or error. If necessary, it should be brought before the church congregation, and, if this fails, treat the person as heathen. The most important thing to remember is the application of discipline; application of human wisdom is hopeless. Unless a person has been born of the Spirit of God, it is not advisable to ask them to settle disputes that arise within the church. Only prayerful planning and Scripture-led instructions should dominate the action of the Church.

The following are the topics of some lessons we should learn from the various churches which Jesus talked about in His revelation to the

Apostle John:

Pergamos	Their following of corrupt doctrine.
Thyatira	Their lack of faithfulness.
Ephesus	Their loss of love toward Christ.
Laodicea	Their lukewarmness.
Sardis	Their works not perfect.
Philadelphia	Blessed for their faithfulness to Christ—they kept his word.
Smyrna	Known for their good works.

RULES OF CONDUCT IN THE CHURCH

Love one another	John 13:34
There should be no division	1 Corinthians 12:25
Be humble	John 13:14
Love is the fulfillment of the law	Romans 13:10
Accept one another	Romans 15:7
Live in harmony	Romans 12:16
Be devoted to one another	Romans 12:10
Serve one another in love	Galatians 5:13
Forgive one another	Colossians 3:13
Pray for one another	James 5:16
Encourage one another	Hebrews 10:25
Love your enemies	Matthew 5:44
Build each other up	1 Thessalonians 5:11
Build up the Body of Christ	Ephesians 4:12

When put into practice, these rules of conduct will either prevent affliction or cure it. Why? Because they are the basic written rules given by God, they are God's own Words. They are based upon the experiences of Christ's apostles—Paul, Titus, John, and others who gave us the Scriptures. To approach the above with a sound mind and love is to lift up Christ and His church.

SOME PEOPLE DEPART FROM THEIR LOCAL CHURCH FOR VARIOUS REASONS

(1) The church is not based upon the Word of God.
(2) The preacher's popularity exceeds Christ's popularity.
(3) The preacher heeds to the whims of the best givers or power heads.
(4) The people are inundated with unscriptural church laws.
(5) The church becomes more social than spiritual.
(6) The church is sinking into a lethargy of indifference.

There may be other reasons. The sooner credence is given to a true conversion, the sooner a true fellowship and effective ministry will begin.

SUPERIORITY OF THE NEW DISPENSATION

To help understand the Church we should look into the record of changes which has taken place over the old Mosaic Law. Hebrews, 8:6,7. Verse 6 tells us that Jesus was given a priestly work, which would be superior to the old covenant, because it is based upon promises of better things. Verse 7 reads, "For if there had been nothing wrong with the first covenant, no place would have been sought for another. [Meaning the new dispensation]."

The first agreement was the covenant of the Law between God and Israel. It was abolished when the second and final covenant, made by God, for all of humanity, was completed at the cross. Jesus' one-time sacrifice ended all other sacrifices. Through this final covenant, God made possible what the old agreement could not, which was, to bring complete forgiveness and full restoration to all who would believe in Christ's one time sacrifice. With the first covenant, it was mandatory to keep every single law which man could not do. To obtain forgiveness for these sins, the High priest would go into the Holy of Holies, a special chamber in the Temple. At this annual event, the high priest would offer blood from goats and bulls for the sins of himself and the people.

It is very interesting to know that when the curtain was torn down in the Temple, it was torn down at the precise moment that Jesus died. This curtain separated the chamber of the Holy of Holies, and the other section of the Temple (Matthew 27:50-51). This was God's way of saying that no longer would any sacrifice have to be made by men because it was being made once by His Son. *This second covenant involves God's grace.* It requires no works, except to believe in His only Son.

THE CHURCH, A SPIRITUAL TEMPLE OF THE SAINTS

The book of Ephesians makes clear the role of the believers, and who the chief cornerstone is. We read this (2:19-22): "Consequently, you are no longer foreigners and aliens, but fellow citizens with God's people and members of God's household, built on the foundation of the apostles and prophets, with Christ Jesus himself as chief cornerstone. In him the whole building is joined together and rises to become the holy temple in the Lord. And in him you too are being built together to become a dwelling in which God lives by his Spirit". God chose to refer to the believers in His Son Jesus Christ, as "saints." They are not saints made by the hands of men, but by the Word of God (1 Peter 1:23).

BECOMING A SPIRITUAL MEMBER OF THE CHURCH

There is only one way anyone can become a spiritual member of the Body of Jesus Christ. It is through a spiritual baptism into His Body. How does one get this spiritual baptism? Just repent and believe upon the Lord Jesus Christ. Repentance is a continuous resolve to correct immoral behavior and lifestyle because of being truly sorry. *Importantly, repentance is not an act or process, by which we make ourselves perfect for salvation.* It is only sorrow expressed, and the changing of one's mind toward sinful living. The process and hope of living a Christ-like lifestyle takes place after a person is saved (John 14:26). It is carried out after a conversion has taken place.

Spiritual immersion into Christ establishes not only a conversion, but also an immersion into a new life. This new life separates the person from his old sinful life, and brings him into the family of God.

THE TEMPLE OF HIS BODY AND WHAT IT MEANS

Believers come into the Temple of Christ's Body upon their conversion from unbeliever to believer. The Body is the Church and

Jesus is its head. Those who come to believe in His suffering, death, and resurrection are then added to the Body (Acts 2:47). The Church was founded and is based upon the Person of Jesus Christ, who was really God manifested in a physical body. Believing this fulfills the written Word about Jesus having been fully God and man. God says, those who do not believe this are the Antichrist. A person like this, according to the written Word is not of God (1 John 4:2,3).

ARE YOU A MEMBER OF CHRIST'S CHURCH?

Are you part of God's family? If not, you can be. To be sure, you must do some thing. Call upon the name of Jesus Christ, and tell Him that you do believe in His bodily resurrection. Then, commit yourself to a turning away from anything which is sin; this is the repentance part which you have read about in chapter 8. Through His Holy Spirit, God will help you do the rest. Remember that it is not that you, all by yourself, make yourself good before God and then He accepts you. It is not a measure of good outweighing bad. It is the commitment that you make to cut yourself off from your old way of life allowing the Holy Spirit of God to have His way with you to help you to grow in grace and in the knowledge of Jesus Christ.

EVERY PERSON WHO REPENTS IS
ADDED TO THE CHURCH

Those who repent and call upon the name of Jesus Christ are saved by God's grace and become spiritual members of Christ's Body. There is a distinct difference between local church role membership and being a spiritual member of the Body of Christ. When we are baptized into the Body of Christ, we become spiritual members of the church. Role membership is a physical status. However, a person should have both. Christians, both ordained and lay people, must realize that the church is not theirs to rule. When Jesus is edified, the church will flourish through the blessing of God, and the Church's mission outreach will please God. In most local churches, the membership roles may consist of both the saved and the unsaved. When "unequal yoking" exists, the spirituality of the church is affected.

JESUS OFFERS ENCOURAGEMENT TO THE CHURCH

"Do not let your hearts be troubled. Trust in God; trust also in me.

In my Father's house are many rooms; if it were not so, I would have told you. I am going there to prepare a place for you. And if I go and prepare a place for you, I will come back and take you with me that you also may be where I am. You know the way to the place where I am going" (John 14:1-4).

CHRIST IS COMING BACK FOR HIS CHURCH SOON

CHAPTER 13

REWARDS

There is something about getting a reward that attracts the attention of almost everyone. I remember my mother used to give me a reward for being a good boy. The reward always had worth, and it always felt good to know that I was in her good grace. That sort of setting has never left me.

There is also the reward for the investor who gets a dividend for his reward. And a Boy Scout who receives his Merit Badge. The carnival prize or reward that goes to the man who can swing the sledge hammer and ring the bell at the top of the post. The salesman who receives a reward for reaching certain quotas. There is a reward for a person who has worked all his life, it is called a retirement check. We receive many different rewards in life. We will receive a reward from God for good stewardship. We should always remember that "Every good and perfect gift is from above, coming down from the Father of heavenly lights, who does not change like shifting shadows" (James 1:17).

Reward is recompense or something we get for doing something special. The Bible refers to reward as something given for either good or bad. Things we do are measured as bad or good.

The Psalmist mentions a reward for the righteous, and punishment for the wicked. (Psalms 58:11, 91:8). *Salvation, though, is not a reward—it is a gift of God.* Man will receive a reward for his works. Matthew 16:27 records that Jesus will reward each according to his works.

SOUL WINNERS REWARD

Daniel (12:3) says, "Those who are wise will shine like the brightness of the heavens, and those who lead many to righteousness, like the stars forever and ever." This is a reward beyond our imagination. Can you imagine the tremendous power which exists in the brightness of the heavens?

159

JESUS TELLS OF REWARDS DUE TO HIS SERVANTS

"And if anyone gives a cup of cold water to one of these little ones because he is my disciple, I tell you the truth, he will certainly not lose his reward" (Matthew 10:42).

"For the Son of Man is going to come in His Father's glory with his angels, and then he will reward each person according to what he has done" (Matthew 16:27).

"Blessed are you when people insult you, persecute you and falsely say all kinds of evil against you because of me. Rejoice and be glad, because great is your reward in heaven, for in the same way they persecuted the prophets who were before you" (Matthew 5:11-12).

Jesus said that whoever welcomes us, welcomes Him. Also, that whoever welcomes God's messenger will share in His reward.

TO THE FAITHFUL STEWARD

The parable or story which Jesus gives us in Matthew, chapter 25, reflects two kinds of rewards. It tells of three men who were each given a certain amount of money. At the end of a given period of time two of them proved worthy. Their investments brought back a very good return. Their master was pleased with all, except one man. He was afraid to do anything with the money, so he put it in the ground for safekeeping. His master, showing his displeasure with his idleness and unfruitfulness, took the money away from him and gave it to the other man who had made the best return on his investment. The lesson to be learned in this story is, yes, you've guessed it, reward. You see, when God gives us something, He expects us to use it to His glory; and He holds us accountable.

After Jesus told the parable about the talents, He said, "For everyone who has [done something with his talents] will be given more, and he will have an abundance. Whoever does not have, [done something with his talents] even what he has will be taken from him" (Matthew 25:29). In principle there were two rewards given. One was for faithfulness, the other for unfruitfulness. It is devastating for any

160

man to lose favor with God. Do we really take inventory every day of all the many blessings God gives us? We should thank Him for every blessing every day.

GOD SHOWS HIS MERCY ON THEM THAT LOVE HIM

God tells us in Psalms about our "giving thanks" to Him. He said, "He who sacrifices thank offerings honors me, and he prepares the way so that I may show him the salvation of God" (Psalms 50:23).

Those who love, honor, and obey God, feel good about themselves. Then they picture God as He is, full of mercy. *His salvation is His mercy.* When we receive His salvation, we know that it is His gift to us. "For the Son of Man is going to come in his Father's glory with his angels, and then he will reward each person according to what he has done" (Matthew 16:27). Those who have not been made right with God through Jesus Christ will receive God's judgment.

BENEVOLENCE

We all hold in high esteem those who are generous. Benevolence is an inclination to do charitable or kind acts. The true altruistic person is one who thinks of others first. A person in this category is usually a well-liked and loved human being. Think back in your life and see if you can remember someone who did something for you, especially at a time when you needed that particular thing most. Gratifying, wasn't it? God used such a man in my life; he put me on the right track in the Word of God. Thus, Jesus came into my life when I needed Him the most. The Lord loves generous givers. God is also a great rewarder to those who diligently seek Him (Hebrews 11:6). God blesses the poor of this world who are rich in faith and want the kingdom of heaven. The faithful are those who obey the law of the kingdom. To love your neighbor is to love yourself. The poor that God refers to are not the financially unsound, but rather the spiritually poor. The spiritually poor are those who know they are insufficient or imperfect when it comes to their spiritual condition before God. (See James 2:5-8).

Each of us has imperfections in one way or another. When we lay our imperfections before the Lord, we then admit our poor spiritual condition before Him, and He will then turn around and bless us for our trust in Him. The proud are puffed up, think they are great on their own, and do not need God.

EVIL DOERS BEWARE

God will reward in a different way those who do harm to His servants. Many faithful pastors in our churches of today experience a great hindrance in their ministry. When the spiritual authority of a pastor is minimized, either through power plays within the congregation or by individuals who want self-gratification, the guilty will receive a reward they may not want. All rewards mentioned in the Bible are not equal. Often, when the pastor preaches a strong and powerful message, people are disgruntled with him, but when he preaches something soothing to their ears, they show their pleasure. Those who take the pastor's authority away from him in subtle ways hinder the works of his ministry; and God will, according to His Word, reward them, but not in the way they are expecting. Alexander the coppersmith, a metal worker, did a lot of wrong to Paul. Paul said, "... The Lord will repay him for what he has done" (2 Timothy 4:14).

RIGHTS OF MAN VERSUS WHAT IS RIGHT WITH GOD

In our country today we are saturated with people who are obsessed with "their rights." I believe in our constitution's authority concerning rights. However, it is quite evident that many people abuse these constitutional privileges when it comes to what is right with God. Perhaps it would be best if we Americans would first base our constitutional opinions or interpretations upon the laws of God and then decide what is best. If this became a common practice, we would not have such unrest and division in our country on so many issues.

God will, however, be the final rewarder for both the right and the wrongs that prevail. He is a rewarder of those who seek Him. It is not our job to pass judgment on others. When we judge others, we find ourselves doing the same thing they do. Then we have no excuse. God will reward those who do good. Paul told the Romans, "But glory, honor, and peace for everyone who does good: first for the Jew, then for the Gentile. For God does not show favoritism" (Romans 2:10).

REWARDS AND THE GIFT OF ETERNAL LIFE

Eternal life is not a reward, it is a gift. After you read this next passage, look at the description written for your examination. "For the wages of sin is death; but the gift of God [not reward] is eternal life through Jesus Christ our Lord" (Romans 6:23).

> *Sins* are either reconciled through Christ or paid back with death (Hell).

> *Death* in a spiritual sense means to be separated from God with eternal punishment.

> *Gift of God* is what it says, a gift, not a reward.

> *Eternal life* "Now this is eternal life: that they may know you, the only true God, and Jesus Christ, whom you have sent" (John 17:3).

> *Jesus Christ is God,* "...I and the Father are one" (John 10:30).

AT THE TRANSFIGURATION GOD SAID, "THIS IS MY SON, WHOM I LOVE; WITH HIM I AM WELL PLEASED"

Transfiguration means to transform or change the figure or outward appearance. This is what happened to Jesus when He went to a high mountain. With Him were Peter, James, and John, the brother of James. Before their very eyes, Jesus was transfigured and was changed in His appearance. His face did shine as the sun. It probably was very difficult for them to even look at Jesus. His clothes were white as light. The three disciples actually saw Moses and Elijah talking with Jesus.

"Peter said to Jesus, Lord it is good for us to be here" (Verse 4). Then a bright cloud overshadowed them and they heard a voice coming from the cloud saying, "This is my Son, whom I love; with him I am well pleased. *Listen to him"* (Please read Matthew 17:1-9).

163

Jesus then instructed them not to tell anyone until after He, the Son of Man, would be raised from the dead. If we could place ourselves in the shoes of these men who were with Jesus, what would we say? They saw Jesus change in His outward appearance. They saw Him in His heavenly glory. They saw Jesus talking with Moses and Elijah. One would think nothing could ever change their faith in what they saw.

They probably recalled what Jesus said to them earlier on. That he would go to Jerusalem and suffer many things. This would be done at the hands of the elders, chief priests, and teachers of the law. Also, that he would be killed and on the third day he would be raised to life (Matthew 16:21). Yet, we know that Peter had denied Jesus three times. My how Peter must have felt! Would you say we have much to be thankful for? The gift of life is there. We just have to lay claim to it and then follow Him. I know many brethren who walk with a deep sense of appreciation and gladness in their hearts to know that Jesus has made it so easy for them. How about you? What are your thoughts on things such as the gift of life, God's forgiveness, and the many rewards that may be awaiting you?

AT CHRIST'S BAPTISM, GOD, AGAIN SAID, " THIS IS MY SON, WHOM I LOVE; WITH HIM I AM WELL PLEASED"

There was another time when God said this very same thing. It was at the beginning of Jesus' ministry. This was after John the Baptist had baptized Jesus. "And a voice from heaven said, This is my Son, whom I love; with him I am well pleased " (Matthew 3:17).

Isn't it good and pleasing to our hearts today to be able to share in such great and amazing Bible truths as this? God is a rewarder for those who diligently seek Him and it is impossible to please Him without faith (Hebrews 11:6). The gift of life is possible only because we believe upon His only Son Jesus Christ.

RICHES IN GLORY

Believers in Jesus Christ soon learn the great joys and peace which come from knowing the God of all creation. When it sinks into our heads that our sins are truly forgiven, and we are pardoned from judgment of our sins, great joy comes into our hearts (John 5:24).

JOINT HEIRS WITH CHRIST

There is a joy and a peace which comes over us when we read what God has promised us in His Holy Bible. Listen to what Paul said in the book of Romans.

"Therefore, there is now no condemnation for those who are in Christ Jesus, because through Christ Jesus the law of the Spirit of life set me free from the law of sin and death" (Romans 8:1-2). God will not judge those who have surrendered their lives to Christ, live by His teachings, and are led by the Holy Spirit.

Read about God's promise in Romans 8:14: "Because those who are led by the Spirit of God are sons of God." The Holy Spirit guides the believer, and God makes the believer His son. (Galatians 4:7).

On being adopted by God; "For you did not receive a spirit that makes you a slave again to fear, but you received the Spirit of sonship. And by him we cry, Abba, Father" (Romans 8:15). The Christian has no more reason to fear because God has adopted him, as a son. Instead, the Holy Spirit now leads the believer. Because the Word of God calls us believers into a "sonship", we know the certainty of our salvation. Would God call us "sons" and then not honor His promise of eternal life? Certainly not, God is not a liar.

About our being God's children: "The Spirit himself testifies with our spirit that we are God's children" (Romans 8:16). "Children", in the Greek is "teknon", meaning one born, a child. God's presence in us assures us that we are His children. God's presence comes into the newly converted child of God at the moment of their conversion. This is when a new spiritual birth has taken place. This is a time when we give our old life to Jesus Christ and receive a new spiritual life.

About our becoming Joint Heirs with Christ. The one who shares in Christ's suffering is a believer, and God declares the believers to be His children. He says they have also inherited a oneness in His Son. Those who believe their sins died with Christ can also believe they will live with Him forever (Romans 6:8). These are the promises of God.

165

We feel the reward of the prize each time we read about God's promises. How about you ? Reading the Bible daily brings confidence.

Example, in this passage, about inheritance, which believers have, is expressed so beautifully and it is truly a treasure to behold. Romans 8:17, "Now if we are children, then we are heirs—heirs of God, and co-heirs with Christ, if indeed we share with the sufferings in order that we may also share in his glory."

About the Glory which is yet to come: Paul said, in Romans 8:18, "I consider that our present sufferings are not worth comparing with the glory that will be revealed in us." Christians will suffer certain consequences when they identify themselves as Christians and refuse to conform to the ways of the world.

God has given us His Word and His Spirit. He keeps believers, as they hope and wait on Christ's return. He helps those who wait for their inheritance. This inheritance is all of the glory we will have when we are with Him forever. To be with Him in His wonderful presence is worthy. Praise be to the God of creation and our salvation! Praise be unto Him who is merciful and just, for He alone is God!

Whoever you are, wherever you may be, think on these things, and may the Lord be with you. I am glad to have shared these things which our gracious God has given, to all who will believe in His Son.

THE REVELATION FROM JESUS TO THE APOSTLE JOHN

"BEHOLD, I AM COMING SOON! MY REWARD IS WITH ME, AND I WILL GIVE TO EVERYONE ACCORDING TO WHAT HE HAS DONE" (Revelation 22:12).

CHAPTER 14

JUDGMENT

Judgment is always difficult to face. God's justice is forthcoming in the Day of Judgment. Man continues to fight the very idea that God will put a judgment on him. Some even deny God, because they think this will allow them to escape His judgment. God has given man very clear instructions through the Scriptures. Man is not without notice of God's love and his judgments. He will find it difficult to deny hearing about either one at the proper time. God instructs us to live godly lives. If these instructions are followed, escape from judgment is ours.

GOD DESIRES MAN TO LIVE PEACEFULLY

Through Paul the apostle, God said, "I urge, then, first of all, that requests, prayers, intercession, and thanksgiving be made for everyone—for Kings and all those in authority, that we may live peaceful and quiet lives in all godliness and holiness. This is good, and pleases God our Savior, who wants all men to be saved and come into the knowledge of truth. For there is one God and one mediator between God and men, the man Christ Jesus, who gave himself a ransom for all men—the testimony given in its proper time" (1 Timothy 2:1-6).

A LOOK AT THE PAST

God rescued a man named Lot from the wicked city of Sodom. Sodom was destroyed because it was filled with evil. Evil from a bad character shows itself as wickedness and will receive God's judgment. All who have not been washed in the blood of Christ will receive God's judgment. In Noah's time God was so displeased with the people of the earth that He flooded the entire earth. All perished except Noah and his family. *The Bible reveals without equivocation that God's justice is forthcoming in the Day of Judgment.*

A LOOK INTO THE FUTURE, WITH SOMETHING TO HOPE FOR

The Day of Judgment will come. "...Their place will be in the fiery lake of burning sulfur..." says God (Revelation 21:8). Even though, many deny the coming of God's wrath, there is hope for those who want to escape His judgment. This hope rests in Christ Jesus. This next passage reminds us of God's fondness for godly people. Godly people are the righteous people, who obey God's Word. "... The Lord knows how to rescue godly men from trials and to hold the unrighteous for the Day of Judgment, while continuing their punishment" (2 Peter 2:9).

GOD WILL SEPARATE THE GODLY AND THE UNGODLY

Judgment for the unbeliever in Christ is inevitable. The day is soon coming when God will separate the godly and the ungodly, the saved, and the unsaved. Scripture reveals, *"He will punish those who do not know God and do not obey the gospel of our Lord Jesus"* (2 Thessalonians 1:8). Many deny that God will do this. Does His Word lie? Can anyone afford to take the chance of not believing that His judgment is forthcoming?

IT IS TIME TO FACE THE TRUTH

The God of all creation, who is Father of our Lord and Savior Jesus Christ, is love. He is not about love... He is love. (1 John 4:8). *God's plan of Salvation, for humankind, is not based upon judgment but is based upon His love for all people in the world.*

WHAT IS YOUR DECISION?

If you have read this entire book, which has expressed God's love and compassion for the people of the world, what conclusion have you come to? If you have refused to acknowledge Jesus Christ as the Savior of the world, and above all your personal Savior, do you think God will spare you?

GOD'S JUDGMENT

Judgment, according to God's Word, will come upon those who refuse His invitation for restoration (2 Peter 2:9). Man either accepts or refuses God's offer. Jesus calls on us to believe upon Him, but many remain stubborn to His call. He's also been patiently waiting for His servants to deliver the gospel message to the unsaved (Matthew 10:7). God's will is that all people be saved through the only mediator between God and man, the man Jesus Christ (1 Timothy 2:4,5).

THE MOST READ VERSE OF SCRIPTURE

I am very grateful to a special friend in Christ who gave me my very first verse of the Bible. "For God so loved the world that he gave his one and only Son, that *whoever* believes in him shall not perish but have eternal life" (John 3:16). I learned to memorize this passage, and more importantly found out the *"whoever"* was intended for me. Do you believe God wants you to be saved? If you are saved, then perhaps you too enjoy sharing the Good News with your family, friends, and neighbors. If not, then remember what Jesus had to say about public confession: "Whoever acknowledges me before men, I will also acknowledge him before my Father in heaven" (Matthew 10:32).

MODERN TIMES VERSUS THE TIMES OF OLD

Is there any advantage to living in these modern times? There certainly is. We have many, many advantages in these times. *If you have turned off your listening to the Word of God, or, if you continue to refuse to read God's Holy Word, you will be missing the greatest opportunity of your life.* The Gospel of Jesus Christ has been spread all over the world, and it has been denied all over the world. The Christian Church and its many outreach ministries have been diligently working throughout the world. Many local churches have grown into basic Bible-believing and Bible-teaching churches; and they continue to labor in bringing the message of salvation to the unconverted.

In 1990, The Gideons International completed their placement of five hundred million Bibles worldwide. These Bibles included over fifty different languages. There is hardly a place of lodging where one does not see the Word of God. The American Bible Society and other organizations have been doing a tremendous job in getting the holy Bible out into the world. Missionaries are working in all parts of the world, spreading God's message of love? Radio programs like Dr. James Dobson's continue to bring Christian living standards to its listeners. The Prison Fellowship ministries under the head ship of Charles Colson have helped millions throughout the world. Billy Graham's evangelistic outreach has touched millions. We are living in a period of God's Grace. Today, we cannot compare ourselves with the dark ages of the past. Opportunities to come to know the love of God through Jesus Christ have never been better.

THE CHURCH AGE—HOW MUCH LONGER WILL IT LAST?

The "Age of Grace" will one day come to an end. And, "... The time will come when men will not put up with sound doctrine. Instead, to suit their own desires, they will gather around them a great number of teachers to say what their itching ears want to hear. They will turn their ears away from the truth and turn aside to myths" (2 Timothy 4:3-4). Where do you fit into this passage of Scripture? There are two kinds of people who may fit into the above passage. First, there is the person who knows that the preacher is talking to everyone but them. Second, there is the person who knows that the preacher is talking directly to them. The wise person will always search their own heart when God's Word about judgment is being preached.

The Holy Bible was not available in the English language prior to John Wycliffe's translation in 1380 AD. It was forbidden to laymen starting in the year 1229 AD. Today, the Bible is available in many languages and many modern day translations. There will come a time when people will not listen to sound doctrine. *We must first listen before we can hear what the Word of God is saying.* It has been said the Bible is the most printed book in the world and the least read. *We are living in a time of God's Grace.* Does the holy Bible play an important part in your life today? Why not make it a daily commitment to study the written Word of God?

STRIPPED OF PARADISE

Adam and Eve were in paradise. They disobeyed God and were removed from paradise. All through the historical recordings of the Old Testament, God dealt with the sins of people. God, however, continued on a course of action to save all people from destruction. His love for all people has been shown through the atoning death and sacrifice of His Son, Jesus Christ. *God has not relinquished His commandment of obedience.* It still applies to all people of the earth, believers, and unbelievers. Paul was concerned with the believers at Corinth. In a letter that he had sent to them, he said, "The reason I wrote you was to see if you would stand the test and be obedient in everything" (2 Corinthians 2:9). It is not possible for the natural or unsaved man to understand the obedience that God requires. When he is converted to a true believer in Christ, the Holy Spirit will help him to be obedient.

NO OTHER PLAN

According to the written Word of God, there are no other plans to save man, other than through the express person of God's Son, Jesus Christ. Scriptures do not disclose any other plans, methods, systems, or sacrifices through which God will restore man or woman to Himself. In effect, Jesus said that the gate to hell is wide and many are heading for it, but the gate and road to eternal life is narrow and only a few will find it. (Paraphrase of Matthew 7:14 mine.)

GOD'S WILL

God's will is not judgment, but salvation. Salvation is the opposite of judgment. *Salvation keeps man from hell.* If man is not saved by God's grace, he will be judged by God's wrath. Does God have both characteristics? He does and we should never forget that He alone is God. Our God, the God of creation, is the One who is "To judge everyone" (Jude 15). However, He would rather have all people be saved, for Himself and from hell (Acts 2:21).

GOD'S WARNING AND GOD'S PROMISE

Paul spoke to the Galatians: "Do not be deceived: God cannot be mocked. A man reaps what he sows. The one who sows to please his sinful nature, from that nature will reap destruction; the one who sows to please the Spirit, from the Spirit will reap life" (Galatians 6:7-8). Those who are truly good don't see themselves as good. Those who incorrectly see themselves as good, fool only themselves. The poor in spirit are those, whom Jesus addressed, saying, "Blessed are the poor in spirit". They are the ones who have come to recognize that they are not self-sufficient, and they know that they need the Holy Spirit's power and presence within them. The proud overlook their sins and justify themselves, by thinking they are good. Wisdom comes to those who trust in Christ. Anyone who remembers what they were like

171

before they became saved know they are dependent upon the Lord Jesus Christ. The peace of God is with those who find Christ.

THE KINGDOM OF GOD

What have you based your salvation on? Some believe their works put them right with God; they believe that their perfect church or church attendance is all they need. They place faith in their financial giving and being good as their ticket to heaven. Jesus said, "Again I tell you, it is easier for a camel to go through the eye of a needle than for a rich man to enter the kingdom of heaven" (Matthew 19:23). A true commitment to trust, follow, and obey Christ should come first, then the other things find their proper place in the life of a Christian.

Jesus told Nicodemus, a teacher of the Old Testament Bible, "I tell you the truth, no one can see the kingdom of God unless he is born again " (John 3:3). How about you? Is this too much of a revolutionary concept for you, as it might have been with Nicodemus? His eyes were focused on the law. *The entrance to the kingdom of God is not through the traditions or the doctrines of men; it is through believing that Jesus is the Christ and inviting him into your heart.*

Paul said, "For the kingdom of God is not a matter of talk but of power" (I Corinthians 4:20). This power is released through the Holy Spirit at the time of man's conversion.

Paul also said, "For the Kingdom of God is not a matter of eating and drinking, but of righteousness" (Romans 14:17). We must not become content with only knowing the right answers about Jesus. We must take on a lifestyle which reflects His power in us. This power rests in knowing we are right with God, and using the fruits of the Spirit's presence. He is the one who will bring a peace that passes all understanding. Though this chapter intends to focus upon God's judgment as it appears in His written Word, it is only fitting to continue to point out the alternatives God gives us in His written Word. Your decision is in your hands. Waiting is not the answer.

THE BENEFITS OF WISDOM

Quality of being wise; knowledge and ability to use it so as to be of value to oneself and others is how Webster defines wisdom. *To come to know God through Jesus Christ is the wisest decision anyone can make for themselves and their loved ones.* In Proverbs, God tells us about a wisdom that saves, "fearing the Lord." God says we are to take His commandments and put them into our hearts. Wisdom comes from God as we ask for it. This is the kind of wisdom worth having.

We are instructed to cry out to God for knowledge and understanding, so that we can know the fear of the Lord. This fear does not refer to being afraid of Him. Instead, it is to come to know His love and will for us. His deep love for you and me is something we need, but often we don't know how to find it. If you don't know it, God wants you to learn His ways. He wants you to develop good insight and understanding which will keep you from doing the wrong things (Proverbs 2:1-11).

JEHOVAH, GOD OF THE MOST HIGH

"Let them know that you, whose name is the Lord—that you alone are the Most High over all the earth" (Psalms 83:18). [The King James Version uses the name "Jehovah"].

God is the creator and sustainer of the universe. His revelations, judgments, attributes, characteristics, His love, and incarnate manifestation are recorded in the Holy Bible. *His greatest creation is man. He made man in His own image. God is love and man has the capability to love.* Man's love is conditional, except when he is converted and regenerated by the Holy Spirit; then man's love is based upon the Spirit's presence in him. (Man here is used generically)

Because of disobedience to God, Adam and Eve lost their place in paradise. The recorded historical events concerning man's depravity or immorality caused God to reveal His anger many times. The Old Testament reveals the ungodliness of man's sinful behavior.

God cannot and will not tolerate sin. Sin separates man from God. Because He is righteous, He wants no part of unrighteousness. God loves man and wants him to choose a way of life that is right and correct with Him. Man was made for God. God was sorry that He made man, and if it were not for Noah, man might not have occupied the earth very long. All through history, man has demonstrated his stubbornness to the laws of God.

God is omnipotent; He has absolute power and authority (Matthew 19:26).
God is omnipresent; He is everywhere (Acts 17:27).
God is omniscient; He knows everything (1 John 3:20).

"God does not show favoritism" (Acts 10:34). He knows the needs of everyone, even before they ask. God calls His people, and He delivers them from doom. He gives certain gifts or talents to everyone. God is sovereign. He is the supreme power and authority. Man can add nothing to what God has already made. *The full revelation and love of God is in Jesus Christ.* Man's only hope of knowing God's love for Him is through Jesus Christ. The limitations of the human mind keep man from understanding the deep mysteries of God, because to him they are foolishness (1 Corinthians 2:14).

God is Spirit, changeless, all powerful, all knowing, righteous, holy, and eternal. His judgments are good, and they are right. His judgments are unsearchable (Romans 11:33).

THE GOOD NEWS (INHERITANCE)
THE BAD NEWS (JUDGMENT)

God has this to say: "He who overcomes will inherit all this, and I will be his God and he will be my son. But the cowardly, the unbelieving, the vile, the murderers, the sexually immoral, those who practice magic arts, the idolaters and all liars—their place will be in the fiery lake of burning sulfur. This is the second death" (Revelation 21:7-8).

WHERE DO YOU STAND BEFORE GOD?

Is your name in the Book of Life? I hope you have read this book with a careful eye and a genuine search for truth. If you cannot answer the question of whether you are saved with a "yes," then you should know this: now is the time to ask Christ into your life; tomorrow may be too late. Don't put it off another minute because it is not a complicated religious process. Just believe in your heart that Jesus Christ was raised from the dead for your justification, and make a solemn promise to yourself, before God, that you will turn away from sin. It is unmistakable according to God's own words that we are saved by Grace through faith (Romans 10:9-10 and Ephesians 2:8). Don't delay; God's Word says, "Now is the day of salvation" (2 Corinthians 6:2).

JUDGMENT OR NOT... WHICH IS FOR YOU?

Listen to what the Word of God says, "Whoever believes in him is not condemned, but whoever does not believe stands condemned already because he has not believed in the name of God's one and only Son" (John 3:18).

There are many today who seem to think their respective position with God is all right. The mindset of so many are not current with what the Holy Word of God is saying. If you are among these, then I encourage you to "get the real thing," and come to the Word of God.

Judgment is inevitable for the unsaved. Do not be foolish and think that some day in the future you will make a change and get serious. Hell will be filled with this kind of thinking. I say these things to help you prepare yourself before God. Man's worst enemy is pride. Look out! Do not let your pride keep you from the best inheritance you will ever get. The benefits are out of this world!

WILL JESUS CONFESS YOUR NAME
BEFORE THE FATHER?

"He who overcomes will, like them, be dressed in white. I will never blot out his name from the book of life, but will acknowledge his name before my Father and his angels" (Revelation 3:5). The saved man, woman, or child will be in white raiment (meaning pure and clean) and be with God forever. Their names are in the book of Life.

THE SECOND COMING OF CHRIST

"Let us rejoice and be glad and give him glory! For the wedding of the Lamb has come and his bride has made herself ready. Fine linen, bright and clean, was given her to wear" (Revelation 19:7). Here, scripture tells us about Jesus, who is portrayed as the Groom, and the

175

Church His Bride. When Jesus comes again this is what will happen. *In the wink of an eye, we will be with our Savior. Jesus is coming for His Bride, the Church.*

Jesus Said "...Moreover, the Father judges no one, but has entrusted all judgment to the Son, that all may honor the Son just as they honor the Father. He who does not honor the Son does not honor the Father, who sent him. I tell you the truth, whoever hears my word and believes him who sent me has eternal life and will not be condemned; he has crossed over from death to life" (John 5:22-24).

During the reading of this book, have you felt the passion of wanting to come out from the darkness of a sinful life? That you want to rid the burden of guilt, troubles and despair that is in your life today. That passion my friend — is the Holy Spirit speaking to you. Jesus Christ is knocking at the door of your very soul asking to come into your heart, to abide in you, to give you peace and the greatest gift you could ever imagine ..... Eternal life!

I WANT TO BECOME A CHRISTIAN, WHAT DO I DO NOW?

Listen to your heart and *open* the door for Jesus, fall on your knees and accept him as your Savior. Talk to Jesus as a friend you want forever, ask Him to come into your heart. Humble yourself before Him because He is Lord, Son of the living God. Ask for forgiveness of *all* your sins. *The Lord God Jesus Christ will forgive you and give you salvation.*

"That if *you* confess with your mouth, Jesus is Lord, and believe in your heart that God raised him from the dead, *you will* be saved" (Romans 10:9).

"I write these things to *you* who believe in the name of the Son of God so that *you* may know that *you* have *eternal life*" (1 John 5:13).

THE VERY WORDS OF JESUS CHRIST
TO ALL WHO BELIEVE IN HIM

"The Spirit gives *life*, the flesh counts for nothing. The words I have spoken to you are Spirit and they are *life*" (John 6:63).

"I give them life, and they shall never perish; no one can snatch them out of my hand" (John 10:28).

MY DECISION TO RECEIVE JESUS CHRIST AS MY SAVIOUR

Having read the Holy Scriptures about Jesus Christ, I know now that I am a sinner in need of God's forgiveness. I want Jesus Christ to come into my heart and change my present life into one of a Christian who believes and follows His word. I now pray this prayer before God.

"Dear Jesus, Son of God, I confess all my sins to you at this very moment and ask for forgiveness. I open the door of my heart. Will you please come into my life and live within me? With your help, I will turn my life around. Jesus, I believe in your resurrection, and now receive you into my life as my personal Saviour and Lord."

My name _____

Date _____

NOW THAT I AM A CHRISTIAN,
WHAT DO I DO FROM HERE ON?

Study the Bible daily. Meditate upon the four Gospels starting with the book of Matthew which references itself to the Jewish prophecies. Then, Mark —is showing Christ as the tireless Servant of God and man. Next, the book of Luke purposes itself in a connected and orderly narrative of the life of Christ as seen by eyewitnesses. The book of John reveals the deity of Christ. This book is a faith builder for those who want to come to know just who the Son of God really is. All other New Testament books will help you grow according to God's Word. This suggested manner of Bible will allow you to grow in the Word of God. Your study of all the Scriptures in both Old and New Testament will bring you into great enlightenment.

Never despair, instead, always pray for God's guidance. Look for other believers to become part of your life, because you have the same Saviour and Lord. When you trust, follow, and obey the inspired Holy Scriptures, you are truly *believing* in the only One who gives life — Jesus Christ, because he is the truth, He is the way, and He is life itself.

177

"IT'S IN THE BIBLE"

HOW OFTEN HAVE YOU HEARD IT SAID, WHERE IS IT IN THE BIBLE?

BAPTISM

Where did it come from?	Matt 21:25-27
Baptism of repentance.	Luke 3:3
Baptism, symbol of burial and resurrection.	Romans 6: 3-4
One body, Spirit, hope, Lord, faith and baptism.	Ephesians 4:4-5
Water baptism: "pledge of a good conscience."	1 Peter 3:21
Jesus said. "... it is proper for us to do this..."	Matthew 3:15

DIFFERENCE IN BAPTISMS:

Jesus will baptize you with the Holy Spirit.	Matthew 3:11
John baptized with water.	Mark. 1:8

CHURCH

The beginning of the Church.	Acts 2:1-2, John:2:19
The Church is the redeemed.	Ephesians 1:7
Jews and Gentiles are one in Christ.	Ephesians 3:5-6

CHRISTIAN LIVING

The Love Chapter.	1 Cor 13:1-7
Life without love is nothing.	1 Cor 13:2
What is perfection?	Ephesians 4:13
Putting on Christ.	Ephesians 4:24
Husband and wives submitting to God.	Eph 5:21-22
Wives submit to husbandd.	Eph 5:24
Husbands, love your wife.	Ephesians 5:25
Christians living.	Mat. Chaps 5,6,7
Holy Communion "Feast of Remembrance."	1 Cor 11:26
Sharing things with your spiritual teachers	Galatians 6:6
How do I put on my spiritual armor?	Eph 6:10-19
How to achieve good goals.	Philippians 4:13
Why without Jesus you can do nothing.	John 15:5
Faith and love are acceptable to God.	Galatians 5:5-6
Why must I have the right religion?	2 John 9
New life, putting on Christ.	Ephesians 4:24
Believers in Christ will be like Him.	1 John 3:2-3

178

How to present yourself to God.	Romans 12:1-3
If you've been given much, much is expected.	Luke 12:48
Submitting to the Lordship of Jesus Christ.	Colossians 2:6
Avoid sexual immorality.	1 Thess. 4:3
Hope of being holy.	Leviticus 20:7,8
Why must we go into prisons?	Matthew 25:
Do not hold back good from anyone.	Proverbs 3:27

FAITH

Faith and belief that Christ is coming for his believers	1 Thess.4:16-17
What is faith?	Hebrews 11:1
Faith comes from hearing the Word.	Romans 10:17
You are justified by faith.	Romans 3:28

FELLOWSHIP AND RELATIONSHIP WITH GOD

Sin looses my fellowship with God.	James 1:15
How am I restored into fellowship with God?	1 John 1:9
The believer in Christ is made secure.	Romans 8:36-39

HOLY SPIRIT

Jesus tells of sending the Holy Spirit.	John 14:26
Receiving the gift of the Holy Spirit.	Acts 2:38
Fruit of the Spirit.	Galatians 5:22
Who teaches us the Word which is truth?	John 14:26
How to fight the battles in this world.	Eph 6:10-19
Speak against the Holy Spirit—no forgiveness.	Matthew 12:32
God anoints Jesus with the Holy Spirit.	Acts 10:38
Believer are sealed by the Holy Spirit.	Ephesians 4:30
Spirit will guide you into all truth.	John 16:13

INFALLIBLE GOD

Christ died and returned to life.	Romans 14:9
One perfect Sacrifice by Christ our Lord.	Hebrews 9:26

JESUS CHRIST

Jesus is the way, the truth and the life.	John 14:6
There is no way to God except through Christ.	John 14:6
Jesus is the Word and is God.	John 1:1-14
The Word became flesh, Jesus Christ is God.	John 1:14
The Word, who is Christ, was in the world.	John 1:10
Jesus shows Himself after His resurrection.	Acts 1:3

179

I am the resurrection and the life.	John 11:25
Unless the doctrine is of Christ, all is in vain.	John 14:6
If you don't have the Spirit of Christ, you're out.	Romans 8:9

JUDGMENT (for good and bad)

No judgment for those who follow Christ.	Romans 8:1
Judgment according to works.	Revelation 22:12
Is hell for real?	Rev 20:10, 21:8
He won't send me to hell? He's a loving God.	Revelation 20:15
If I am saved by grace will I be condemned?	Romans 8:1

LAW

The Ten Commandments.	Exodus 20:1-17
God's greatest commandment.	Matt 22:37-38
God's second greatest commandment.	Matthew 22:39

OBEDIENCE

"Obedience that comes from faith."	Romans 1:5
Those led by the Holy Spirit are sons of God.	Romans 8:14
To pray, be clear minded and self-controlled.	1 Peter 4:7
Christ's obedience did it all .	Romans 5:18-19
"Every thought to make it obedient to Christ"	2 Cor 10:5
Obedience more important than sacrifice.	1 Samuel 15:22
Always be right with God and don't shrink back.	Hebrews 10:38
Don't turn back to old principles.	Galatians 4:9
Jesus was obedient to God until He died.	Philippans 2:8

PARADISE

Today you will be with me in paradise.	Luke 23:43
Tree of life in the paradise of God.	Revelation 2:7

PRAYER

The Lord's Prayer.	Matthew 6:9-13
Jesus prays alone.	Mark 1:35
Jesus prays for all future believers.	John 17:20
Master key to prayer.	John 15:7
Lifting up hands in prayer.	1 Timothy 2:8
Two agreeing in prayer.	Matthew 18:19
Prayers of a righteous man.	James 5:16
Prayer without doubting.	James 1:6
Praying without ceasing.	1 Thess 5:17

Asking according to His will.	1 John 5:14
Prayer before eating.	1 Timothy 4:3
How prayers are heard.	Hebrews. 5:7
Prayer power when two agree.	Matthew 18:19
Why we should pray without doubt or wrath.	1 Timothy 2:8
Christians — with a new attitude.	Ephesians 4:23

PROMISES

What God will do when you serve Him.	Exodus 23:25
How can I know Jesus really wants me?	Rev 3: 19-20
Where in the Bible does it say, He forgives?	Ephesians 1:7
God's promise of eternal life.	1 John 2:25
Your place in heaven, prepared by Jesus.	John 14:2

SALVATION

Is salvation necessary?	John 3:3
How you can be Saved.	Romans 10:9-10
Born again.	John 3:3
God's love for mankind.	John 3:16
Salvation sealed by the Holy Spirit.	2 Corinthians 5:5
Personal salvation ... when?	2 Corinthians 6:2
Redeeming the time.	Colossians 4:5
Should I ask God to save me now or later?	2 Corinthians 6:2
Is "Born again" in the Bible?	John 3:3
Once a believer, a new creation in Christ.	2 Cor 5:17
By grace are ye saved through faith.	Ephesians 2:5-8

SIN

What is sin?	1 John 5:17
Don't fool yourself about sin.	1 John 1:8
Sin against the Holy Spirit—no forgiveness.	Matthew 12:31
Deliberate sinning.	Hebrews 10:26
Sin comes with our birth.	Psalms 51:5
The Holy Spirit gives power to keep us from sinning.	Romans 8:13

TRUTH

God's Word is truth.	John 17:17
Who wrote the Bible.	2 Timothy 3:16
Warning about changing the Bible.	Revelation 22:19
The power of the Word.	Hebrews 4:12

How you can recognize the Spirit of God.	1 John 4:2
How to tell the spirit of an antichrist.	1 John 4:3
The Spirit guides believers into the truth.	John 16:13
The truth will set you free.	John 8:32
The Holy Trinity. 1 John 5:7 (KJV)	Matthew 28:19
Does the Church get me into Heaven?	Ephesians 2:8
The Word of the Lord stands forever.	1 Peter 1:25
Through God's Word the earth was formed.	2 Peter 3:5
God's Word will not return empty.	Isaiah 55:11
You are in error if you don't know the Scriptures.	Matthew 22:29
How to have peace with God.	Philippians 4:4-7
Knowledge of truth.	I Timothy 2:4
Believer is set apart, sanctified forever.	Hebrews 10:14
The Lord gives us understanding.	2 Timothy 2:7

WARNINGS

Warnings about taking away from the Word.	Revelation 22:19
Spirit of the Antichrist.	1 John 4:3
Ignore Jesus Christ and you don't have God.	1 John 5:12

WITNESS

Witness in earth	(KJV)	1 John 5:8
The Great Commission.		Matthew 28:19
The Gospel.		1 Cor 15:1-4
The power to witness.		Acts 1:8
God's command to witness.		Matt 28:19-20
What is the Gospel we must witness to?		1 Cor. 15: 1-4
How to witness.		Luke 12:12
Be prepared to witness.		1 Peter 3:15
Every believer has the ministry of reconciliation.		2 Cor 5:18
Believers have the witness in them.		1 John 5:10
It is wise to save souls.		Proverbs. 11:30
The beginning call to all believers to fish.		Matthew 4:19

WORSHIP

How to glorify God.	John 15:8
How do I worship God?	John 4:24